RELIGIOUS
ABUSE

A PASTOR EXPLORES

THE MANY WAYS

RELIGION

CAN HURT

AS WELL AS HEAL

KEITH WRIGHT

RELIGIOUS
ABUSE

A PASTOR EXPLORES

THE MANY WAYS RELIGION

CAN HURT

AS WELL AS HEAL

Northstone

Editor: Michael Schwartzentruber
Proofreading: Dianne Greenslade
Cover and interior design: Margaret Kyle

Unless otherwise noted, all quotations from the Bible are from
the New Revised Standard Version, copyright 1989 by the Division of
Christian Education of the National Council of Churches of Christ in the
USA. All rights reserved. Used by permission.

Quotations from the Revised Standard Version of the Bible, copyright 1946,
1952, and 1971, by the Division of Christian Education of the National
Council of Churches of Christ in the USA.
All rights reserved. Used by permission.

Northstone Publishing acknowledges the financial support of
the Government of Canada, through the Book Publishing Industry
Development Program, for its publishing activities.

Northstone Publishing is an imprint of Wood Lake Books Inc., an employee-
owned company, and is committed to caring for the environment and all
creation. Northstone recycles, reuses, and composts, and encourages readers
to do the same. Resources are printed on recycled paper and more
environmentally friendly groundwood papers (newsprint), whenever possible.
The trees used are replaced through donations to the Scoutrees for Canada
program. A percentage of all profit is donated to charitable organizations.

Canadian Cataloguing in Publication Data
Wright, Keith, 1931-
Religious abuse
Includes bibliographical references.
ISBN 1-896836-47-X
1. Control (Psychology) – Religious aspects – Christianity. 2. Self-
actualization (Psychology) – Religious aspects – Christianity. I. Title.
BV4597.53.C62W74 2001   248.4   C00-911523-4

Published by Northstone Publishing,
an imprint of Wood Lake Books Inc.
Kelowna, British Columbia, Canada
www.joinhands.com

Printing 10 9 8 7 6 5 4 3 2 1
Printed in Canada by
Transcontinental Printing

DEDICATION

I am grateful to the congregations I served over the span of 37 years and I dedicate this book to them. They allowed me to search and grow as a pastor and teacher. They were willing to ask difficult questions and not expect pat answers. They saw the Christian faith as a journey, not a destination.

They were not perfect and neither was I. They would recognize the abuses I have described in this book and they would admit that we were part of an institution that often betrayed the One we sought to serve.

But, for the most part, they were people of great compassion. They demonstrated their love for God, not by doctrinal correctness, but by serving people in need. They were people with open hearts, open minds, and open hands.

To the people of First Presbyterian Church and St. Andrew Presbyterian, in Lake Charles; First Presbyterian Church, in Lubbock; and Faith Presbyterian, in Austin; I say, "Thank you for joining me in a spiritual journey. May you hear and accept the commendation of Jesus, 'Well done, good and faithful servants, enter into the joy of your Lord.'"

CONTENTS

FOREWORD

I love the church! It has been a wonderful combination of mother and father and, as such, carries within it all the feelings such a family dynamic might suggest. As an Episcopal priest and professor of pastoral theology at a seminary, I have spent my entire professional life caring for the church, nurturing it, and reacting to it. Like other institutions, it is wonderfully human and fits all the requirements of any gathered community. More often than not, it does its work magnificently and in a manner worthy of its call. Other times, however, the church behaves in ways that produce profound discomfort and grievous consequences. Because the church holds the love and deep affection and traditions of many people, the effect of such bad behavior can be genuinely tragic. Keith Wright is a child of the church and its faith. In this important book, he moves to de-mythologize the abuses of power within church communities and asks that the institution move to re-examine itself.

Why is this book so important?

Most of us have been reared to believe that when God or the church is mentioned, our response must always be positive, else we are not faithful folk. Thus, a fearful guilt or even recoil is likely to accompany any criticism – as though to disagree is to shake a fist at God. The church tends to define God with great certainty, and any human disagreement is thus condemned with certitude as well. Too often, what is missing is that the church refuses to be reflective. It avoids criticism and seems to prefer to put out questionable truths rather than risk having its behavior questioned or its power reined in. Predictable enough results occur when the human institution we call the church ignores its own brokenness and evades its own need for forgiveness. Indeed, something truly terrible happens – the church wounds; the church is oblivious to the pain; the church turns a deaf ear to questions; the church protects itself at all costs. In short, when the church is compelled always to be right, those who have a differing view are hung out to dry.

Such behavior is not worthy of an institution called to compassion and mercy.

To raise these questions or to attempt to do something about these circumstances requires courage. Keith Wright's work embodies that courage. He has thought about this for a long time. A gentle man, Keith has written this book out of his loyalty and affection for the church. The results are as straightforward as a handbook. Keith asks the church to review itself, to raise questions about how it behaves, and to ponder those issues with fidelity as it attempts to guard the tradition that defines its responsibility to the world in the first place.

Karl Rogers, the eminent American psychologist, used to say, "The facts are friendly." No one needs to avoid the truth, even the truth about oneself, even when the truth is hard. The church needs to face the facts presented here.

William C. Spong, D.D.

PREFACE

In many ways I owe my life to the church. I had never stepped inside a church until I was ten years old. My father had been excommunicated from the Roman Catholic Church and my mother was too ill to take me to her church. I spent four years with an aunt and uncle who also did not go to church. When I returned home after my mother's death and my father's re-marriage, it was my stepmother who introduced me to the church. I was an only child living with a father I had seen only occasionally for the last few years and a stepmother whom I hardly knew. In this situation, I found in the church what I needed at that point in my life – an extended family of aunts and uncles and cousins and grandparents who surrounded me with their love. I also heard of a gracious God who loved me so much that "He was willing to send His Son to reveal His love and to die for my sins." I was obviously too young to question the theological and biblical assumptions and the paternalist language which were the foundation of what I was hearing. At that moment, the church and its message were what I needed and I was grateful for it. In fact, I was so grateful for what the church and the Christian faith had done in my life that I decided, while still in high school, that I wanted to go to our denominational college and become a minister.

With that gratitude in mind, it must seem rather ungrateful now to write a book that is critical of religion in general and the Christian church in particular. Let me make it clear; I write not to join the chorus of those who are quite sure that the church is dead and who are simply waiting for a proper burial. As long as people gather together to share a common faith, some institutional form of that faith will be inevitable. Therefore, if the Christian faith were to fade away and the churches closed their doors, something else would rise up to take its place and that new institution would be just as fallible and flawed as what it replaced.

I write, instead, as a pastor who feels compelled out of his own experience to call attention to the ambivalent nature of the church. Yes, the church has done some wonderful things in society and in the lives of individuals, but the church has also been a destructive force in society and in the lives of people. The evidence is too overwhelming to deny that religion has a dark side as well as a light side. I believe that all who are connected with the church know this deep down in their hearts. The problem is that no one wants to confess it in public and thereby take responsibility for making changes that would *increase* the church's ability to bless and *decrease* its ability to hurt.

As I wrote this book, I felt like the little boy in the story of the emperor's new clothes. When the emperor appeared naked in public after having been duped by swindlers who convinced him that they were weaving him a new suit, his subjects were afraid to say what they saw. Finally, a little boy cried out, "The emperor doesn't have any clothes on." Everybody knew that, but they were afraid to tell the emperor the truth. Everybody knows that the church has been guilty and is still guilty of much evil, but very few people within the church are willing to tell the truth. A friend who is a professor of evangelism once called me an evangelist. I was shocked because that wasn't an image I held of myself as a pastor. However, I understood what he meant when he went on to say that my passion was to reclaim those who had left the church, those who had been hurt by the church, those who could no longer believe what the church teaches. There are millions of people who long for a relationship with God, but who cannot find that relationship in a church that will not own up to its limitations, its mistakes, its failure to put peace and justice and love ahead of self-interest and success and doctrinal correctness. There are millions of thinking, caring people in the church right now who find it hard to remain in an institution that will not take seriously its own faults and flaws and the abuse that it heaps upon its members. It is to these people and their spiritual leaders that I write in the hope that they will start a dialogue which will take seriously the problem of abuse in every religious institution and begin to do something about it.

1

RECOGNIZING RELIGIOUS ABUSE

My father was a kind and gentle man – a man who, I was told, once thought about going into the priesthood when he was a young boy. His father died when he was ten and being one of the older boys, he had to leave school in the fifth grade to go to work to support his mother and the rest of the family. That pretty well ended Dad's dreams of being a priest. However, I'm quite sure that his devotion to the Roman Catholic Church would never have waned had it not been for the fact that he fell in love with a young lady who was a member of a Protestant denomination called the Disciples of Christ. When they decided to get married, she refused to become a Roman Catholic and my father had to decide between his religious roots and the woman he loved. Fortunately for me, he chose my mother. He agreed to be married outside the Roman Catholic Church and to suffer the consequences of banishment from the sacraments, and thus from what he had been taught was the means of his salvation.

A few years later, my mother developed tuberculosis. About the same time, she joined the Christian Science Church. As a small child, I remember hearing my father late at night pleading with my mother to seek medical treatment for her illness. At one point, she *did* agree to enter a sanitarium in the higher, drier climate of west Texas. With medical attention and a favorable climate, she might have recovered, as did her sister who had the same illness and who stayed at the clinic. However, members of the Christian Science Church traveled to west Texas to persuade her to return home near the coast and to trust that God would heal her. She died when I was seven.

As I look back upon my father's and mother's experience, *I am convinced that they were victims of religious abuse.* The religious community where Dad found faith and solace and meaning and a relationship with God as a child could not tolerate a love relationship which challenged its authority. So it tried to force compliance by the threat and ultimate decree of excommunication and damnation. The members of another religious community pursued his young wife relentlessly when she dared to challenge their narrow concept of how God works in healing. She died as a result of their dogmatic and authoritarian approach to religion and I am sure my father was convinced that they were responsible for her premature death. My father was rejected by the religion of his childhood, which could brook no dissent. And he was robbed of many years with a woman he loved, when my mother's life was cut short because of a religion that took the legitimate affirmation of God's power to heal, but forgot that God uses medical science as a part of that healing process.

My father and mother would never have called their experience religious abuse. There was no name, back then, for what happened to them. My mother died and Dad simply lost any enthusiasm for organized religion. He was a good father to me and a faithful and loving husband to my stepmother, whom he married two years after my mother's death. He went about silently helping people in need. He attended and finally joined the Presbyterian Church, where my stepmother and I worshipped. But I know that he did it primarily to please us.

As I look back over 37 years of ministry, I have become convinced that all of us, myself included, have suffered one form of religious abuse or another. Thankfully, the abuse that many of us have suffered is not as dramatic or as damaging as that experienced by my father and mother. But the abuse is there nonetheless. Religion is the institutional expression of a divine/hu-

man encounter and because the human beings who
make up that institution are imperfect, the religious
community they create will have the capacity not only
to bless but also to abuse those who are a part of that
community.

Almost 25 years ago, Wayne Oates saw this destructive and abusive side of religion and wrote about
it in his book *When Religion Gets Sick*. Dr. Oates has
taught at Southern Baptist Theological Seminary as
well as at Wake Forest College, Union Theological
Seminary, and Princeton Theological Seminary. In
his book, he gives over 50 examples of people whose
religion led them to do very destructive things to
themselves and others. From these examples, he concludes, "These instances convince us that the term
religion is very ambiguous, and that, like the word
love, it covers a multitude of sins. It can refer to a
very positive, health-giving doctrine by which men
[*sic*] not only survive but live and do well...At the
same time, religion can refer to a pantheon of false
gods by which men [*sic*] shrivel in the bondage of
fear and death."[1] Oates continues his observation
about the dual nature of religion as he writes:

> *These questions imply that religion may be either*
> *sick or well and that it is not always one or the*
> *other. Ordinarily, it is sick in some respects and*
> *well in others at the same time* [emphasis mine].
> This view keeps us from the intellectual dead

ends of Freud's assumption that religion is a universal neurosis at all times and places. It also avoids the sweet optimism of denominationalism in American religion; that is, that religion, because it is religious, has to be well, good, and healthy by the nature of the case. Both kinds of thinking are unrealistic and do not fit the facts of life.[2]

The term religion, then, can have both a positive and a negative connotation for each individual.

Gregory Baum, a Roman Catholic theologian and sociologist, writing five years later, speaks of the ambiguity of religion. Baum contrasts the negative and positive aspects of religion. On the negative side, he reminds us that religion often legitimates the existing power relations. On the positive side, he points out that religion is often the glue that binds a community together. Thus he comes to the conclusion that "If all these things are true, then religion must be a many-leveled, complex and ambiguous reality."[3]

Actually, religious ambiguity is nothing new. Baum points to the biblical record as evidence of good and evil residing side by side within religion from the very beginning. He writes:

The Bible paints a highly ambivalent picture of religion [emphasis mine]. The faith of the people is ever threatened by various religious trends that undermine their openness to divine truth and falsify their understanding of the human world. It is possible to read the Scriptures as a textbook on the pathology of religion. The prophets of Israel offer us a detailed critical description of the corrupting religious trends; we learn from them to distinguish idolatrous religion, superstition, hypocrisy, legalistic religion, and finally religion as a source of group-egotism and collective blindness. So vulnerable is the religion of God's people that it is in constant need of redemption; the believing community remains in need of the divine Word which continues to judge its religion and renew it in terms of greater trust, surrender and fidelity.[4]

Howard Clinebell, founder of the Institute for Religion and Wholeness at the Claremont School of Theology, writing more recently, echoes both Oates and Baum as he agrees that it is not a case of religion being *either* sick or healthy. *Actually, it is both at the same time.* In his book *Well Being*, Dr. Clinebell writes, "The religious life of most of us (I would say all of us) is a paradoxical blend of pathogenic (abusive) and salugenic (saving) aspects, of limiting and liberating spirituality."[5] Clinebell quotes a friend who once said to him, "Religion can be either a set of wings with which our souls fly or a lead weight around our necks!"[6]

As I have listened and talked with both those inside the church and those who have given up on organized religion, I have found that it is never an either-or but rather a both-and situation. Religion is for each of us *both* a set of wings *and* a weight around our necks. Each person will experience it more as wings than weight or vice versa, but it is never purely one or the other.

That may sound strange, but it will begin to make sense if we come to think of religion in the same light that we think of our parents. All of us need to give up the idea that our parents are perfect. Some parents are a lot better than others, but none are perfect. Our parents both bless us and wound us. They give us life and they teach us great truths which enable us to live happy, productive lives. But they also teach us things which are untrue and which make our lives less than they could be. They nurture us and enable us to grow and think for ourselves. But at times they threaten removal of their love if we disagree with them and thus they make us anxious and insecure.

If we are fortunate, we receive more blessing than wounding; if we are unfortunate, the opposite is true. But no matter how fortunate we are in being blessed by loving, caring parents, there is some aspect of abuse present. And no matter how unfortunate we are in being cursed by selfish, immature, abusive parents, there is probably a strand of life-giving love to be found. If we are fortunate, we are able to stay within the family circle because the abuse is tolerable and the benefits of the love we receive outweigh the damage done by the abuse. If we are unfortunate, the abuse is too great and too threatening, and when we realize what is happening, we must leave the family as soon as possible, perhaps never to return, or to return only when our parents are willing to seek counseling and to become less abusive.

What I have just said about parents can also be said about religion in general and the particular religious community where we worship. We need to give up the idea that religion is perfect – that the church of which we are a part is perfect or infallible. Religion, like our parents, has the capacity to bless us and to wound us and it inevitably does both at different times.

Now, if that is true, we can rejoice in the good that we receive from our religious community, but we can also begin to identify where religious abuse has been hurtful or damaging in our life, and where it has stood in the way of our own spiritual development. Only when we are aware of the capacity of religion to abuse can we guard against that abuse and take steps to curb it where it exists. Only when we recognize the ambiguity of our own religious community can we assess the merits of remaining a part of that community or of leaving it. We make our choice to stay or leave based on the relative weight of the abuse versus the nurturing love we find there. We may choose to remain in the community and, as a mature adult, refuse to be victimized by the abuse we have identified. We can also do everything in our power to make the religious community aware of its abusive behavior or belief system in the hope that it will change.

Still another alternative open to us is to look for a religious community that is more loving and caring and less abusive. This is where the analogy of our relationship with our parents obviously breaks down, because, ordinarily, switching parents is not an option except in the rarest of circumstances. However, in appraising our religious family's strengths and weaknesses, this option offers a way to avoid religious abuse without dispensing altogether with religion itself.

Hopefully, as leaders and members of the religious community, we can become more aware of abusive behavior in our own setting and take steps to minimize it. We can work to build a community where love outweighs abuse and where spiritual growth and development can take place. If that is not possible, we can search for another faith community where it *is* possible. And even in those cases where we have been hurt too deeply to remain within the religious circle, we can remain open to divine love which is always available to us.

Religious abuse exists and, therefore, I am convinced that just as it was necessary for child abuse, spouse abuse, sexual abuse, and abuse of the elderly to be exposed for what they are, so it is also necessary for religious abuse to be exposed for what it is. For centuries, we denied all these other forms of abuse just as we will be inclined to deny the existence of religious abuse. For ages, we assumed that children should be obedient and that this gave parents the right to use whatever force, physical or mental, they deemed necessary to control their children. The beating or berating of a child was considered simply a matter of gaining control for the purpose of healthy discipline. Now we know differently and we recognize that mental or emotional or physical abuse of a child cannot be accepted. In the same manner, for centuries we failed to acknowledge wife abuse because we believed that a woman should be subservient to her husband and that he could use whatever emotional or physical force was necessary to bring about her compliance to his will. Slowly, we are beginning to realize that that kind of thinking can no longer be accepted. No husband or wife has the right to beat or berate his or her spouse as a means of asserting dominance or control and we now call such behavior what it is – spouse abuse.

Likewise, we must begin to look at some of the ways in which religion has dominated and controlled and hurt people and we must call it what it is – religious abuse. We can no longer ignore religious teachings which instill fear or a deep sense of worthlessness and shame, or incite to violence those who come under its influence. Just as we have progressed to the point where we can recognize and admit that other forms of abuse exist, we must also recognize the existence of religious abuse.

When we began, in the last 15 years, to take these other forms of abuse seriously, we discovered that they were far more widespread than we could have imagined. The statistics are shocking, almost unbelievable. Last year in the United States 2.7 million children were reported abused. It is estimated that one in every four girls and one in seven boys will be sexually abused by the age of 18. Thousands of battered wives seek safety in women's shelters. One woman out of every three can expect to be sexually assaulted by a parent or relative or date or some other male during her lifetime. In the last few years, we have become more and more aware of elderly people who are abused by their own families, or by staff in nursing homes.

When we finally admit that religion can also be abusive, we will discover that all of us have been abused to some degree. Some who have been more severely abused will be relieved to know that the anger and guilt and fear and feelings of worthlessness which consume their lives are not of their own making, but rather the product of an imperfect religious community which badly wounded them. As we begin to talk about religious abuse, we will discover its many forms and we will begin to identify what has happened to us and to label it for what it is.

While I was a pastor, I heard scores of unsolicited stories about harmful religious experiences which wounded people badly. As I have talked with people recently about writing on the subject of religious abuse, many have come forward to talk about their own experiences. I am sure that other pastors have had similar experiences, or that they *will* have similar experiences when they open their eyes to the problem and give people a chance to talk about what has happened to them.

But, unfortunately, people don't always talk to their pastor about religious abuse. Quite often they are so turned off or frightened by their pastor, who may be part of the problem, that they turn to a psychiatrist, a counselor, or a neighbor and pour out their feelings of perpetual guilt, fear, and anger which has come from their religion. Scott Peck, in his book *The Road Less Traveled*, tells the story of Kathy, a person who was deeply abused by her religious upbringing. Then he says, "There are millions of Kathys. I used to tell people only somewhat facetiously that the Catholic Church provided me with my living as a psychiatrist. I could equally well have said the Baptist Church, Lutheran Church, Presbyterian Church, or any other."[7] My conversations with other psychologists and psychiatrists and counselors have confirmed Peck's estimate that there are millions of people who suffer from religious abuse.

Only when we begin to recognize the existence of religious abuse can we do something about it. Only when religious leaders and members of religious communities admit that religion can abuse as well as bless, can they even begin to address the problem. Only when our consciousness is raised and we confess that some of the things that we teach and some of the ways we treat people within the faith community are harmful and destructive, can we as clergy and lay leaders begin to amend our ways. Just as parents can be abusive without being conscious of it, so too can the religious community wound rather than heal, reject rather than include, burden rather than lift the load that weighs us down, without even being aware of what they are doing. We must be willing, therefore, to examine what we do and teach to see whether it is abusive or not.

This will not be easy, because there is so much resistance to self-criticism within the structures of religion. While few religious teachers or leaders would claim infallibility or the absence of impure or mixed motives, there is a great reluctance to admit publicly the ambivalent nature of religion, or to tolerate those who question the teachings and the social and moral pronouncements of the church.

Fortunately, however, there is a small but growing number of people both inside the religious establishment and in other disciplines who are raising our consciousness about this grave problem. Since 1980, a significant body of literature has been published on this subject. Some of that literature is found in psychological journals, but many articles are also found in religious journals. Just recently, David Johnson and Jeff VanVonderen who are pastor and counselor in a Lutheran church in Minnesota wrote a book called *The Subtle Power of Spiritual Abuse*. In it they tell of their own frequent encounters with abusive behavior or thought forms. They say, "Witnessing the spiritual anguish caused by dynamics like these time after time is what led us to coin the term spiritual abuse."[8] Actually, they were not the first to use the term spiritual abuse, and the mildly apologetic way in which they approach the subject will undoubtedly turn to a much more forceful denunciation as the depth and magnitude of the problem is brought to light.

Having said this, we must admit that the likelihood that swift changes will occur in the behavior of major religious groups or denominations is not very good. Institutions change very slowly and with great resistance. Even if someone had raised the issue of religious abuse to the Roman Catholic Church in the 1920s when my father was opting to marry a Protestant, there would have been no possibility that it would have changed its opposition to his marriage unless my mother agreed to raise their children in the Roman Catholic Church. Forty years later, in the 1960s, a Roman Catholic priest joined me in officiating at a wedding that was held in the Presbyterian church which

I served. The groom on that occasion was Roman Catholic and the bride a Presbyterian. That was both a joyous and a sad moment for me – joyous because it demonstrated how far the Roman Catholic Church had moved from its earlier rejection of my father, and sad because it came 40 years too late for him.

The issue of homosexuality provides another case in point. Despite a growing body of scientific and sociological evidence indicating that sexual orientation is genetically determined, many people in the church continue to believe that homosexuals *choose* their orientation, which they see as sinful. As I grieve over how the changes in the Roman Catholic Church came too late for my father, I cannot but wonder if sometime in the near future my own Presbyterian denomination will ordain practicing homosexuals as officers and clergy. If I am still alive when that time comes, I know that I will rejoice in the acceptance of their full personhood in the community of the faithful, but I will grieve over all those fine people I know who had to leave our denomination to find warmth and acceptance and a place to serve in some other communion – people for whom the change came too late to keep them in the faith community they loved and longed to serve.

Because religious leaders and denominations move so slowly, it is necessary, now, for some within the religious establishment to help offended persons recognize their abuse so that they can begin the healing process. It was impossible for the Roman Catholic Church in the 1920s to recognize how it was abusing my father. Yet someone needed to help him distinguish between the religious community that abused him and the God whom that religious community so imperfectly represented. Sensitive pastors and lay people today must reach out to that vast group of people who have left the church because of religious abuse, as well as to the vast number of people *within* the church, and help them distinguish between the religious community that abused them and the God who will work with them and who is embodied in caring people who take their tragedy seriously.

Religious communities that have become aware of this problem must be willing to confess publicly that abuse occurs and invite those who are victims of religious abuse to give the church a second chance. Then, they must strive to demonstrate in their community an inclusive, nonjudgmental love, which opens the door to a restored relationship with God. They must offer a theology of hope and acceptance to a people who have known only an image of God which was narrow and restrictive and vindictive. They must offer a community in which questioning and exploration are welcome and where the religious experience is viewed as a lifelong journey with God. They must also be willing to form support groups for those who have been most deeply wounded by sexual or psychological abuse within the faith community.

It is no easy task to work with those who have suffered religious abuse. They have been wounded and betrayed by the very institution in which they thought they could find understanding and trust and protection. They will, therefore, be suspicious and wary of *any* religious community. Like battered children, they will need a special measure of consistent love. They will need to hear the pastor and the members of the religious community acknowledge the ambivalent nature of religion; they will need to hear them ask for forgiveness when the religious community does not measure up to the gracious love of God.

It will be difficult to overcome the mistrust of those who have been deeply abused by religion, but the effort must be made! It must be made because God's love is most effectively communicated and made real in community. It is certainly possible to love God and others and oneself without being a part of a faith community, but a solitary relationship with God is a poor substitute for the love of God that can be demonstrated and nurtured and sustained and corrected in our association with a group of fellow believers.

I am convinced that the religious community is an essential part of God's effort to bring wholeness and health to a broken world, and to broken lives. However, for the religious community to be a healing, reconciling agent in society and in individual lives, it must recognize that it has the capacity not only to bless and to heal and to bring people together in love, but also the capacity to wound, to divide, to alienate, and to mislead. Only as it acknowledges its ambivalent nature can the religious community confess its betrayal of God's love and ask God for the wisdom and will to do better. I invite you, then, to explore the abusive side of religion, not so we can dispense with religion, but as a way of making us ready to accept God's help so that we can be part of a healthier, more life-enhancing community.

In the chapters that follow, I will take a long, hard look at the areas of abuse the church must address. So that you can see where I am heading, I will give you a preview of the road we will travel. In Chapter Two, I will share with you some different types of religious abuse I have encountered in my own ministry. In Chapter Three, we will explore two forms of abuse that are so subtle we would hardly recognize them, even though they can cause great pain and mental suffering. In Chapters Four and Five, we will look at the violent side of abuse as it is expressed in sexual and physical abuse of children and women, and at how religion often contributes to both. In Chapter Six, I will challenge the exclusivity of the Christian faith and suggest that it is the ultimate form of religious abuse. In Chapter Seven, we look at the other side of the coin of religious abuse and consider the many ways in which clergy and their families are abused by members of the church they are serving and by higher ecclesiastical authorities. In Chapter

Eight, we will move on to examine some of our basic theological doctrines and I will contend that some of those doctrines need to be changed if we are going to make real progress toward the elimination of religious abuse. In Chapter Nine, I will speak to those who are too badly wounded to ever trust a faith community again and to those who cannot find a faith community that recognizes its complicity in religious abuse and its potential for helping in the healing process. Finally, in Chapter Ten, I will speak to the despair which this kind of examination of religious abuse can create and how we can move beyond that despair to identify and affirm that which is good and healthy and redeeming in the religious community.

This is where we are going in our exploration but before we begin it would be well for me to offer my own definition of religious abuse as background for what I will say later.

DEFINITION OF RELIGIOUS ABUSE

Religious abuse occurs when a religious group or parent or leader crushes the spirit of an individual by substituting dogma or a particular belief system for a continuing and growing awareness of the divine presence. It occurs when religious teaching or preaching justifies violence or the domination of one person or persons by another person or persons. It occurs when religious teaching or preaching heaps unmanageable burdens upon people rather than offering to share their heavy load. It occurs when religion engenders fear and self-loathing rather than liberating people from fear and bondage, enabling them to most effectively love and serve themselves, others, and the God who created them. It occurs when a religious group or leader claims to have the final revelation of God and calls upon people to reject the religious experience of those who believe differently from what the group or leader teaches.

Some of the results of religious abuse will include the following:

- alienation from God and the religious community causing deep anxiety, emotional trauma, psychological distress, and even suicide
- child or spouse battering or verbal assaults
- ridicule or rejection of scientists whose discoveries challenge the prevailing religious community's understanding of the world
- holy wars and death for many people who take opposing religious views
- domination of females by males
- domination of children by parents or parent substitutes
- domination and destruction of animals and nature by human beings
- domination of minorities by majorities
- domination of the poor by the wealthy
- domination of the powerless by the rich and powerful.

2

EVERYDAY
ENCOUNTERS
WITH ABUSE

Even the most cursory review of the history of the Christian religion substantiates the existence of religious abuse of the most obvious and violent kind. Crusades, religious wars, inquisitions, pogroms, witch hunts, persecution of scientists who questioned the church's teachings, and denigration of women all come quickly to mind and remind us that religious abuse can lead to death and terrible hardship.

During the writing of this book, two incidents of deadly religious abuse captured the attention of the public in a dramatic way. In April, 1993, attention was focused on Waco, Texas, where cult leader David Koresh armed his followers for a pitched battle between the forces of good and evil in anticipation of the imminent end of the world. The fiery conclusion to the standoff between the Branch Davidian Cult and the FBI is burned in the memory of all who watched that scene on television knowing that many children were among the 79 persons who died in that inferno.

Four years later, the television again recorded in graphic detail the suicide of 39 members of the Heaven's Gate Cult in California. Once more, a group of people became convinced that their leader, Herb Applewhite, had discovered religious insights which no one else possessed. With complete confidence in their leader, they committed suicide in an attempt to shed their earthly containers and join him on an intergalactic voyage to a "Higher Place." The memory of Jim Jones and the mass suicide of over 900 people in Jonestown, Guyana, in 1978, has not faded enough for us to fail to see the similarities and to learn again what happens when people put their trust in a charismatic religious leader who stifles dissent and demands unthinking and uncritical allegiance from his followers.

Illustrations of dramatic forms of religious abuse abound even though they may not have been labeled as such. The problem is that these more dramatic examples can lead us to conclude that abusive religion is confined to bizarre incidents that make the headlines of today's newspapers. Or we may believe that religious abuse is something that happened long ago and far away – the bloody incidents of the past, which are recorded in history books. So let me share with you some up-to-date, everyday encounters with religious abuse which come from my own experience as a pastor.

Several years ago, a man and his wife came to Austin and worshipped with us for a few months. The man (I will call him David*) was a professor and was on sabbatical leave from the college where he taught in the history department. David had just finished a book that was scheduled for publication. Because he had some free time before he returned to his teaching, we visited on several occasions and talked about history and theology, two interests we both shared. We continued to correspond after David returned to his teaching and one day he sent me a copy of a sermon his pastor had preached. In the letter which accompanied the sermon, David made it quite clear that the little boy in the pastor's story was none other than himself.

The sermon began as follows:

One morning a little boy – a real little boy – a little boy who now lives in a very large and real man, bounded outdoors to play. The sun was brilliant. The air was warm with summer. And for once the boy's brother was not around to compete for the family wagon. There was only one play-wagon for the boys; their father

*All names of people reporting abuse in this and following chapters have been changed.

was a country pastor, and in that time and place even one play-wagon approached extravagance. So the little boy towed the wagon to the top of the hill. With the whole universe beaming on him, he climbed in and pushed off. All by himself! A glorious ride! Drunk with joy, the little boy said, "I'm going like hell!"

The words had no sooner left his lips than the little boy saw his father – not in person, probably, but in his mind. With the vision of his father, a dark shadow fell on his day. The little boy had forgotten himself in gladness. He had used an evil word, a "Devil's word." The ride came to an end in a gloom of guilt. The boy tugged his wagon around behind the house to the manure pile that was there, found a piece of broken bottle, and, in an extravagance of self-blame, tried to cut off his toes.

With a lot of counseling which continued well into his adult life, this son of a Congregationalist minister was able to deal with that awful burden of guilt and ultimately to lead a very productive life. The counselor enabled David to see that he was an abused child – not in the usual sense of physical or sexual abuse, but in the sense of religious abuse.

My professor friend internalized the message of guilt, while a woman I know stood her ground and would not be intimidated. Maria attended Catholic schools during her childhood and youth. She told me about the nuns who frequently rapped her knuckles when she misbehaved in class and who told her and her classmates that they would go to hell if they did not shape up. One day, being a little more feisty or assertive than most teenagers, Maria looked at one of the nuns and asked, "And where are you going?" The nun pulled herself up tall, looked down on the teenager and said, "I'm going to heaven!" At that point, this young girl thought to herself, "If you are going to heaven, I don't want to be there." When Maria was old enough she left the church. Only after many years did she find her way back into a religious community.

Unfortunately, a lot of people do not have the self-confidence or courage to challenge their religious leaders. Many cringe in mortal terror of damnation and hell fire, which they hear preached forcefully from an early age. This was the case with another of my parishioners who told me that, as a young child, she feared that she would die before she made her profession of faith and that she would go straight to hell as a result. Helen was a shy child who could not bring herself to walk down the aisle alone during the altar call, so years passed before she finally found the courage to make that profession of faith. During all that time, she lived in mortal fear.

The fear subsided once Helen made her profession of faith and was baptized as a teenager. But her problems with religious abuse were not over. She left her small home town and the Baptist church where she had worshipped and went away to a large university. There Helen met and dated for three years a young man who was a Jew. He opened her eyes to a wider understanding of God and she began to question the exclusiveness of her Christian faith. When Helen went to her Baptist minister to talk about her expanding horizons, he quickly assured her that her boyfriend was headed for hell and that she should break off the relationship. There really was not anything to discuss as far as the preacher was concerned. It was an open and shut case – anyone who did not believe in Christ was damned. Either she give up her relationship with this Jew, or she, too, was in danger of God's wrath. Helen walked out of that conversation and did not return to a Christian community for some 19 years. At a moment of spiritual growth and the opening of new horizons, this college student had the door slammed by a pastor whose narrow view of God's love excluded all but those who believed as he and his religious community believed. Helen could not accept that narrow viewpoint and kept searching until she found a faith community where questions were acceptable and where faith was more of a journey of continuing discoveries than a point in time marked by a particular doctrinal affirmation.

Then there was the couple who worshipped with us for some time before deciding to commit themselves as active participants in our congregation. I was surprised when the husband asked if he could be a part of our church without officially joining. When I began to explore the matter with him, Sam revealed a history of religious abuse during his youth – abuse which kept him from ever wanting to be totally identified with the church, despite the fact that he participated in worship and other activities quite regularly.

I learned that Sam's father was an alcoholic who had often left the family penniless because of his inability to hold a job. Neither his father nor his mother went to church, but they sent Sam and his brother to a nearby congregation where religion became important to the two boys, if only because they could often bring home food from church socials. When their father abandoned them and their mother died, the two boys, who were 14 and 13, were placed in a foster home with an older couple. These foster parents lived on a farm and two strong young men were seen as a great asset because they could perform many chores. The couple were deeply religious and strict about the observance of the Sabbath, but their religion did not produce warmth and love and acceptance for two young boys who had never experienced these gifts. When this foster home did not work out, Sam and his brother were placed with another couple who owned a chicken ranch. Once again, they were exploited for the free labor they provided and, as was the case with their first foster parents, their new guardians were deeply religious, but devoid of any warmth or caring for the boys.

Surprisingly, despite the joyless, loveless religious home and church which Sam experienced, he became a religious fanatic. At school he was called "The Rev" by his classmates. He read and memorized a good portion of the Bible and even challenged the school principal on a matter of scriptural interpretation during a school assembly. Sam got to the point where he could take no action, including crossing the street, without praying to God about what he should do. The acceptance and warmth which Sam could not find in family or church he found in an authoritative and magical religion which he believed would keep him from all evil and harm.

The bubble of this authoritative religion burst for Sam when he was 19. He was attracted to a young girl of 16 who asked him to take her to a dance in a nearby town. He agreed after arranging for the girl to stay with his sisters after the dance, and after obtaining permission from the girl's mother for her to go. However, when they arrived in the nearby town, the girl asked him if he was man enough to take her to a hotel. Feeling his manhood challenged, but also feeling that God would protect him from any temptation, Sam agreed. When they closed the door to their room, the young girl began to press her warm body next to his and Sam began to pray. She won, and, as far as Sam could tell, God lost. This began a long period during which Sam felt that God was power-less and religion impotent.

Sam is now in his 60s. In the years which have intervened since that night in the hotel, he has begun to understand God differently, but he still has a healthy skepticism about religion. He is well aware of the false and destructive messages which it often gives to young and old alike. He now knows that all religious communities are made up of very fallible human beings, some of whom exploit the powerless; who speak much about the love of God, but who often fail to embody that love and care to others; who prefer a God of rules and magic to a God who empowers us to make decisions based upon respect and care for ourselves and others. I hope that Sam will someday embrace again this very fallible faith community with eyes wide open to its shortcomings and the damage it can wreak. But I also hope that he will be able to recognize the times when it is faithful, when it cares lovingly for the dispossessed and powerless.

Over the years, many people have shared with me not only the positive side of religion, but also its dark and negative side – a side which includes the more violent forms of physical and sexual abuse which we will explore later. I have shared first a few less violent examples, because they receive very little attention in spite of the fact that they cause great pain and suffering and alienate many people from their religious community and, in some cases, from their Creator.

In later chapters we will have to deal with the more extreme forms of abuse, but before we do that, I invite you to explore with me two subtle and less obvious manifestations of religious abuse.

3

TWO SUBTLE
FORMS OF ABUSE

One of the greatest compliments ever paid me as a
pastor came from a young mother who said, "You
taught me to say, 'No.'" She wasn't talking about saying no to drugs or to some other evil. She was talking
about saying no to me, the pastor, and to other leaders in the church who asked her to do one more job.
This woman was exceptionally talented and compulsive about doing everything she was asked to do in
the church. Martha had been raised in a Baptist home
where she had been taught that you never say no when
asked to do something in the church. But, a few years
ago, she found that teaching full time at the high
school level, being a mother to two small children,
being a companion to a husband who was a college

professor, and trying to do everything she was asked to do in the church were about to lead her to a nervous breakdown. She couldn't do everything she was asked to do and, much as we needed her in key leadership positions in the church, I knew that we were asking too much. So I told Martha that she needed to learn to say no, not only at church but also at school and at home. I advised her to seek counseling from a person I believed could help her. With the aid of the counselor, she began to see that God did not demand every second of her time – the church and school and home might, but not God.

Martha reminds me of a woman I met while I was still in seminary. I was working with the youth group in a local church and this woman and her husband were the youth advisors. One evening when I was taking her home from a meeting, she said, "This is the 13th evening in a row that I have been at the church. My husband says it's getting to the point he's going to have to ask me for a date in order to see me."

Overworking people, always demanding more and more of a person's time and energy, is very definitely a form of religious abuse. The origin of this particular abuse can be traced to a misconception of scripture, to the workaholic nature of most preachers, and to the constant demand for bigger and better programs in the local church. To address this manifestation of abuse, we must be willing to examine all three of these root causes of the problem.

It is possible to quote several passages of scripture which seem to indicate that God demands our undivided attention, time, and effort. One in particular comes to mind immediately. Jesus said, "If any want to become my followers, let them deny themselves and take up their cross and follow me" (Matthew 16:24). Other passages which point in this same direction can be found, and some ministers use them to spur their members on to ever greater efforts, oblivious of the other demands and needs which may be present in a person's life at a given moment.

All scripture must be interpreted by the whole message of the Bible and, therefore, no one passage stands alone. Jesus *did* call disciples to deny themselves and follow him. But he also taught us to love others *as we love ourselves* and he said, "Come to me, all you that are weary and are carrying heavy burdens, and I will give you rest. Take my yoke upon you, and learn of me... For my yoke is easy, and my burden is light" (Matthew 11:28–30). One teaching of Jesus seems to contradict the other and this reminds us that we must see each teaching of Christ in the light of his whole message. Jesus was primarily concerned about people – about lifting their burden – about bringing joy and happiness to those whose burden in life had become too great. He poured scathing rebuke upon the religious leaders of his day, whom he said, "tie up heavy burdens, hard to bear, and lay them on the shoulders of others; but they themselves are unwilling to lift a finger to move them" (Matthew 23:4). Jesus challenged people to give their best in any task. He called men and women to follow him and to serve in God's kingdom. But he was always sensitive to the needs of those who were already over-burdened and eager to take a part of that burden upon his own shoulders.

Having said that, we also need to say that in most churches people can be found who have time and energy, and who need to be challenged to teach and serve and lead in the local church. People can be identified who are so wrapped up in themselves and their needs and desires and ambitions that they have no time for the needs of others, or for communion with God in worship. These people need help to see that life is found in giving it away.

The problem is that people who have been taught to feel guilty about everything will automatically feel that *they* are the ones who must heed the pastor's call to service – no matter how much they are already doing and how many obligations they have in other areas of life. If you belong to that large group of compulsive, guilt-ridden people, talk with your pastor and tell him or her how you feel, how you take every word from the pulpit about serving God as aimed directly at you. You need to let your pastor tell you that it's all right to rest, to take time for yourself, to enjoy life, to take care of your own needs.

Don't ever worry that you will not do your part. When I told the young woman whom I mentioned at the beginning of this chapter, to learn to say no, I knew that there was no danger she would ever become self-indulgent and do less than her best at work and in the family and in the church. She had been programmed to do her best and I knew that she wouldn't suddenly change. What I hoped was that she would take some tiny steps toward allowing herself to turn down a few of the things she was asked to do.

I know how she functions because I have been programmed in the same way, and so have most other clergy. It is very hard for us to say no, to relax, to take time for ourselves or for our families, to stop and enjoy life. We can always see one more thing that needs to be done, one more need that must be met, one more cause that must be championed. If we pastors are ever going to address this particular form of abuse, we will first have to admit that we are workaholics who drive ourselves and others because *we* have never learned to say no – *we* are still trying to earn God's favor by our many deeds rather than accepting the grace of God which is freely given.

In the last few years, I have tried to practice what I preached to Martha and I have succeeded to some small degree. However, I never had any fear that I would become lazy or unproductive. All I ever thought I could do was learn to say no occasionally and not feel guilty about it. That is at least a starting point until I can learn that God and others are not dependent upon me to do everything.

That's what Martha needed to learn. She also needed to learn one other very important thing. She needed to learn to distinguish between the needs which God laid before her and the tasks which the church asked her to do. Sometimes those needs are synonymous, but quite often they are not; the work of God and the work of the church are not always the same. If we can keep this distinction in mind, we will experience a lot less guilt and perhaps be able to avoid being abused by our religious community.

Some of what the church does is an extension of Christ's ministry to those in need of spiritual nourishment or physical help. When we are asked to do our part – not to carry the whole load, but just to do our part – we need to listen carefully to the call. If we have the talents, resources, and physical and emotional energy to respond to that call, we need to give it deep consideration. The choice, however, is always ours. Only we know what burdens we already carry. No pastor or religious group has the right to speak for God, threatening divine wrath if we fail to answer a call to service. And ultimately, if we have discovered the compassion and grace of God, we will hear the call as an invitation rather than as a command, and know that we are free to accept or reject it without fear that God will reject *us*.

Religious communities have an unfortunate and abusive habit of burdening people with more than they can handle, but the abuse does not stop there. After laying heavy burdens upon their people, some religious leaders picture a God whom human beings can never satisfy, no matter how much they do – a God who regards our puny efforts as hardly worth a comment, and certainly not deserving of praise, lest we be filled with pride and think that our efforts really count for something. *This failure to give positive reinforcement is, I am convinced, another form of religious abuse.*

Let me give you a picture of what I mean. A woman was referred to me for counseling. Jane was a very good student in her childhood and youth and brought home excellent grades. When she showed her report card to her parents, her mother would respond with obvious pleasure and offer verbal commendation on her daughter's accomplishment. However, when the report card was handed to her father, he appraised it with a stern look on his face and handed it back to her with no comment at all. Jane spent her whole life trying to please her father, trying to elicit just one word of commendation or expression of delight in her accomplishment, but to his dying day, he never acknowledged any sense of pride in anything she did.

We marvel at the callousness of a father who never praised his daughter. Surely this was child abuse, as much as if he had beaten his daughter with a stick. Yet when *God* is portrayed as a stern father or judge who can never be satisfied with our efforts, we often fail to recognize this as religious abuse. Our efforts, according to this image of God, are always flawed or imperfect. Therefore, we are doomed to try again and again but always come up short.

Preachers are often long on criticism and short on praise. Another woman told me about a time in her life when she was caring for her children and her mother who had recently suffered a stroke. She often came to worship exhausted from the endless tasks of the week, looking for a word of encouragement and strength to carry on. Unfortunately, what she heard was her pastor telling her all the things she had left undone, all the things she had only partially done, and how she ought to give more of herself in the service of others. She was confronted with the image of a heavenly parent whom she could never please and who always demanded more.

This woman came close to a nervous breakdown and even to suicide. Fortunately, she found a counselor who helped her realize that God knew what a good job she was doing. The counselor enabled her to see that God was aware that she was exhausted, that God wanted to walk beside her, to lift her burden rather than add to it.

As I look back on my preaching, I realize how often I have fallen into the trap of portraying God as a parent who is never satisfied with our efforts. Yet I know better. I know better for two reasons. *First*, I know from Jesus' own example and from what Jesus taught us about God, that God is pleased by our efforts to do those things that bring happiness and fulfillment to ourselves and others. God is pleased when we live up to our potential as best we can. God offers congratulations and commendation for our accomplishments.

In the parable of the talents found in Matthew, Jesus pictures a God who is delighted by our efforts, a God who says, "Well done, good and faithful servant...enter into the joy of your Lord" (Matthew 25:21). God is like a colleague of mine who was a school teacher before she went to seminary. Her greatest thrill as a teacher came when a light went on in a student's mind and she knew that the student had grasped an idea that had previously been elusive. At that point, she said that she felt like shouting, "Let's throw a party. Let's celebrate your accomplishment!"

I have no doubt at all that when we do things that bring happiness to ourselves or others, when we give up old destructive habits, when we help someone in distress, when we learn to enjoy and preserve the beauty of nature around us, when we hug a child, when we hug each other, when we do a thousand and one things that show we have learned how to love ourselves and others and God, God shouts, "Isn't this great! Let's throw a party!" Wasn't that exactly the reaction of the father of the prodigal son, when his son came to his senses and returned home? Didn't the father shout, "Let's throw a party!"

That's also how we see Jesus in his relationship to his disciples. Those 12 men who made up the inner core of Jesus' followers must have tried his patience mightily! They constantly misunderstood his message. They bickered and fought among themselves right up to the end. Yet Jesus was patient with them, waiting until the light dawned upon their minds, and he was always quick to celebrate any accomplishment.

Once, Jesus sent the disciples out two by two, to preach the good news of the kingdom and to heal the sick. When they got back, they reported their successes with great enthusiasm. And Jesus commended them for the good work they had done. Then, recognizing that they were mentally and physically exhausted, he took them apart to a private place for a well-deserved rest (Mark 6:6–13, 30–32).

This leads me to the *second* reason why I know better than to think that God constantly heaps negative criticism upon us. As the great teacher, Jesus knew that positive reinforcement is far more effective than negative criticism. The most effective teachers are those who know how important it is to praise their students when they have mastered a concept or grasped an idea or completed an assignment.

I have seen this approach work miracles with my grandson who had a learning disability in the first grade. He struggled to learn, but to no avail. He would beat his head with his hand in frustration. Then, in the second grade, he had a teacher who saw the potential in him. She found a method of teaching that he could grasp. But most of all, she praised him for small accomplishments, and, as his confidence grew, she challenged him to attempt more difficult assignments. He went from Special Education in the beginning of the second grade, to honor roll in the third grade and most improved student in the whole school. This transformation came about because a teacher found the method that suited his style of learning, but even more importantly, because he felt her love and praise, and with renewed self-confidence he worked very hard to master the tasks which she assigned him.

As I see how well this approach works, I wonder why preachers and leaders in the church are so slow to follow Christ's teaching and to say much more often to their congregation, "Well done! Your Lord is greatly pleased with what you have accomplished! Let's throw a party to celebrate!"

The general absence of such positive reinforcement has led to the popularity of Norman Vincent Peale, Robert Schuller, and others who emphasize the power of positive thinking. They offer a much needed corrective which is often ignored by many religious leaders because it seems to omit any kind of criticism. However, positive reinforcement does not require that the teacher or the preacher avoid correction or criticism altogether. There are times when we need to be told that we have grown lazy, or that we have hurt others or ourselves, or that we have grown blind to the needs of others. There are times when we become arrogant or rude or thoughtless and we need to hear of God's anger and great sorrow over our behavior. There are times when we need to know that God is displeased with us and that our actions will lead to grave consequences for us and others. *But* this word of correction, of displeasure, of warning, is most likely to result in a radical change when we have heard repeatedly of the delight which God takes in us and in our accomplishments and growth.

Radical change which leads to real growth comes about when we feel the loving affirmation and acceptance of God. This reinforces our own desire to give up self-destructive behavior and to move on to actions and attitudes which bless our own lives and the lives of others. Superficial change and apparent growth come about when we feel coerced into doing something differently by the threat of punishment or the withdrawing of approval from someone significant in our lives.

The problem with hell fire and damnation preaching is that it does nothing to develop inner discipline and strength of character. It only works on those who fear being "caught" doing something wrong. The problem with a religion that provides no positive feedback is much the same. We may continue to work hard but we work from a sense of duty rather than from the joy of knowing that what we are doing is cherished and appreciated by the Creator of all things.

If religion has become a burden to you, if you feel that God is a tyrant who can never be pleased no matter how hard you try or how much you do, you need to know that is not the biblical picture of God – it is not the God whom Jesus came to reveal. In every religious community there needs to be a balance between the challenge to grow and the need for rest, between the push to move on to the next goal and the celebration of what we have already accomplished, between praise and positive criticism. If the balance is not there for you, don't let that community limit your understanding of God. Accept Jesus' invitation: "Take my yoke upon you, and learn from me...For my yoke is easy, and my burden is light." Also, hear Jesus saying to you, "Well done, good and faithful servant...enter into the joy of your master." In that good news you are free to grow and blossom and to serve as the opportunity and your strength allow.

4

RELIGION
AND ABUSE
OF CHILDREN

Several years ago, a psychologist called to ask if I
would lead a private graveside service for a two-year-
old child who had been killed by his father. The
woman who called was the court-appointed counselor for the sister of the boy who had been killed. She
wanted the little girl to have an opportunity to say
goodbye to her brother away from the glaring spot-
light of the press and all the attention that her brother's
death had received. The service was held at a small
cemetery, with only the little girl, her grandparents,
and the counselor present. I had read much about
the case in the local paper, but being asked to help
that little girl deal with her grief and her terror brought
the subject of child abuse forcefully home.

Since that time, I have been appalled at the frequency with which other cases of violent abuse of children have been exposed. A member of the church I served works for the Travis County Child and Protective Services. She comes home exhausted and depressed by the staggering number of cases which she and her staff must handle each day. She supervises seven people who make up one of five units working in the area of child abuse in this county. Each of those units investigates approximately 1,800 reported cases of child abuse each year. Out of the 9,000 cases which these five units handle, about 772 children will be removed from their homes and placed with relatives or in foster homes.

If one reads or watches television and if one thinks at all, it is almost impossible to ignore the magnitude of the problem of child abuse in society at large. Yet many people still believe that their own faith community will be immune to this problem. How could child abuse exist in a community where members and leaders are dedicated to the love and protection of children? How could a respected clergyperson or Sunday school teacher or youth leader or choir director or scout master or officer of the church molest a child? We know the answer, of course; they are human beings like the rest of us and they have their weaknesses and twisted and perverse thoughts like everyone else. But we often overlook that fact and we refuse to admit that child abuse could actually take place in our own community.

I understand this reluctance to face the possibility of child abuse so close to home. I was as negligent as any. Several years ago a couple joined our church. They had a two-and-a-half-year-old daughter. I noticed that the father came to the morning worship service, but the wife stayed home with the daughter. At first, I thought that Sally did not know that young children are involved in the first few minutes of our worship service and are then dismissed and cared for by volunteers. I concluded that Sally was like a lot of parents who do not want to sit through an hour-long service with a bored, squirming child. When I told her about the arrangements we had made for children, I was astonished by her reply. She told me her reason for not bringing her daughter to worship was that she did not want to send her for the better part of an hour to be with adults whom she did not know. She was afraid that her daughter might be sexually abused by one of those adults.

My first reaction was one of amazement. What a silly, overprotective mother this was! How could she possibly believe that some member of our congregation would actually sexually attack a child during the worship hour, with the parents sitting just a few hundred yards away in the sanctuary? When I voiced my amazement, she reminded me that she was a psychologist who had seen too many cases of child abuse to overlook the possibility that it could happen anywhere, and that membership in a church did not guarantee that a person was not a molester of children. She asked if we had done any background checks on our volunteers. I had to admit that we had not, even though I knew that our church daycare center routinely did background checks on those who were hired to work with children during the week. It had not even occurred to me, or to those who were in charge of finding volunteers for this program, that such a check was necessary. We had assumed that a person of strong faith, as we knew our members to be, would never inappropriately touch or molest a child. The thought had not crossed our minds that a child in that program could possibly be in any danger.

Since my conversation with Sally several years ago, many denominations have recognized the danger which this mother brought to my attention and have published guidelines for churches which give advice on how to reduce the risk of child abuse in the church. In addition to this, some churches have written their own policy statements. Covenant Presbyterian Church in Austin, Texas, developed its own guidelines which were adapted from a book provided by the insurance carrier for their congregation.[1] It is interesting to note that the church's policy statement cites two reasons for its adoption by the Session: 1) to reduce the risk that children and youth attending

Covenant's programs might be abused, and 2) to reduce the potential liability of Covenant if an abuse did occur. Not only does abuse occur in church settings, but churches can be held legally accountable for that abuse if proper precautions have not been taken.

The Roman Catholic Church is learning that fact the hard way, as evidenced in an article in the March issue of *America* magazine, a publication of the Jesuit Fathers of the United States. In the article, Andrew Greeley, a Chicago priest and sociologist, estimates that between 2,000 and 4,000 Roman Catholic clergy in the United States have abused young people, with their victims numbering well in excess of 100,000 people. He also states that the cost of treatment, lawyers, and liability settlements is running at $50 million and rising. Extrapolating from the report on abuse cases in the archdiocese of Chicago, Greeley estimates that the number of priests who are sexual abusers could be anywhere between one in 10 and one in 20. In the book *Lead Us Not Into Temptation,* Jason Berry recounts in great detail the molestation of several boys by a Roman Catholic priest in Louisiana. The story is revealing, not only about the fact of child abuse in a religious setting, but also about the reluctance of the hierarchy of the church to acknowledge and deal with the problem. Berry writes: "The crisis in the Catholic Church lies not with the fraction of priests who molest youngsters but in an ecclesiastical power structure that harbors pedophiles, conceals other sexual behavior patterns among its clerics, and uses strategies of duplicity and counterattack against the victims."[2]

On April 4, 1993, the Sunday edition of our local newspaper carried an article with the headline: "SYSTEMATIC PERSECUTION." The first paragraph of that article read, "In a dark episode of Quebec's postwar history, as many as 8,000 children were falsely declared mentally retarded, and many of them were then mentally, physically and sexually abused by the nuns who ran the orphanages where they lived, according to hundreds of people who have publicly said they were victims of the abuse." After reading this article in the morning, I had a conversation with a gentleman later that afternoon in which he mentioned his own abuse in a Southern Baptist orphanage. He told me of a punishment for wetting his bed when he was 11 years old. The house parents made him strip naked and run through a gauntlet of his peers, who beat him with belts as he passed them.

Unfortunately for the Roman Catholic Church, it has gotten the most press when it comes to child abuse. I know of no data that would indicate that the percentage of priest abusers is any greater than that of clergy abusers in any other religious group. Furthermore, it is important to note that all who write on the abuse of children in religious settings are quick to point out that the vast majority of clergy and professionals in the church have never engaged in child molestation; therefore, we must be careful not to raise unnecessary fears.

Still, we keep two things in mind. *First, we are naive when we assume that a clergyperson or leader or member in any denomination or religious group is above abusing a child.* While we must guard against a cynicism that leads us to suspect every clergyperson or choir director or youth worker of the worst, we must also be alert to the *potential for abuse* which is always present when children are in the care of adults – especially adults who have the opportunity to build close and intimate relationships with those who are too young and too powerless to defend themselves. Only when we are aware of the possibility of danger, can we take the steps which will lessen the likelihood of child abuse in our religious community.

This awareness will cause us to be observant, to listen to our children, to teach them that religious leaders and members of the church have no more right than anyone else to touch them inappropriately. We will take complaints of children seriously and investigate them thoroughly. We cannot protect our children from every danger, but we can be vigilant and ready to act if evidence suggests that abusive behavior exists.

Second, we need to insist that those who supervise the work of clergy and staff on every level (sessions, boards, vestries, bishops, presbyters, district superintendents, de-

nominational leaders) take accusations of child abuse very seriously and investigate them thoroughly and quickly. This is important both for the accused and the accuser. When abuse is substantiated, we must also insist that the clergyperson or lay leader be removed from all contact with children and not be allowed to return to his or her responsibilities until treatment has been completed and competent judgment has been made that further abuse will not occur. It is not enough simply to transfer an offender from one parish to another, or to give an offending lay leader a good recommendation for another job in order to be rid of the problem ourselves. To confront the problem demands courage and strength, but to fail to deal with the problem is to put other children at great risk. That would be a tragedy.

Child abuse *does* happen on church property or during church retreats or in other settings where children are in the care of clergy or staff or members of the congregation. *But the more frequent incidence of child abuse in a religious setting is found in the families who are affiliated with the church.* Once again, one cannot assume that because the father in a family is an officer of the church, or that because the mother is a Sunday school teacher, these parents are incapable of abusing their own children. In fact, those who write about the abuse of children point out that religion, instead of deterring child abuse, can actually foster it in many cases.

That may sound unbelievable but listen to the stories. Phil Quinn was an abused child who told of his own traumatic childhood in the book *Cry Out! Inside the Terrifying World of an Abused Child*. In a later book, *Spare the Rod*, he talks about what leads to child abuse and he shares his own insights into this frightening world. He writes:

> Too many parents are willing to do just about anything to their children if they believe it is a good and desirable thing *or that it is God's will* [emphasis mine]. Some parents even believe that it is their Christian duty to administer physical punishment – to build character, discourage sin, and instill a sense of submission and obedience to the will of God, as represented through parental authority. They take what God has created in his [*sic*] own image and refashion it so their children will grow up to be just like them! They think they must tame children as they would domesticate wild horses, so they will quietly take their places in society – a society that must serve the will of the masses through those few.[3]

Then Quinn adds these terrifying words:

> Almost invariably, abusive parents will justify their actions on righteous grounds. They most

often appeal to a higher principle, such as religious duty or love of their child. Their attitude is that anything is acceptable as long as it
is done in love. My adoptive parents told me
hundreds of times, during endless beatings,
that they loved me. *If that was their way to love,
they very nearly loved me to death*! [emphasis
mine][4]

Phil Quinn was lucky. He escaped with his life from
beatings which were justified by appeal to scripture
and to religious instruction. Others are not so lucky.
Philip Greven, in his book *Spare the Child*, tells the
story of two-year-old Joseph Green who died of shock
and hemorrhaging after being paddled for two hours
by his parents. Interestingly, the jury that tried the
case in 1985 ultimately held Dorothy McClellan responsible for the death of the child rather than his
parents. Why? Because McClellan was the founder
and leader of a religious community called Stonegate,
where Joseph's parents had worshipped and where
they had been brainwashed into believing that child
obedience must be enforced, when necessary, by rea-
sonable corporal punishment. Greven quotes the
judge's statement at the sentencing of the defendant:

Dorothy McClellan is an extremely strong-
willed and manipulative woman who was un-
questionably the leader of the Stonegate group.

She instituted therein a policy of child discipline which ultimately encouraged the acts
which brought about Joey Green's death, and
thus is just as responsible as if she had wielded
the paddle herself. One only has to realize that
her teachings created an atmosphere in which
each set of parents had their own mono-
grammed paddles, which were carried openly
and used frequently. Indeed, through her leadership there evolved a system of child abuse
which was mistakenly justified under the guise
of religion.[5]

The fact that Dorothy McClellan was found guilty
and that the Supreme Court refused to review the
case is surprising, Greven concludes, in light of the
fact that McClellan was not teaching some new doctrine of child discipline. Rather, she was simply push-
ing to the limit what generations of Christians have
advocated for centuries. If the judge had considered
how widespread was the Christian church's advocacy
of corporal punishment in breaking the child's will
and in bringing the child into submission to the parent who represents God, the imprisonment of Ms.
McClellan would have been much more difficult.
What if the judge had turned to the Book of
Deuteronomy, a part of the Christian scripture, and
read these words:

If someone has a stubborn and rebellious son
who will not obey his father and mother, who
does not heed them when they discipline him,
then his father and his mother shall take hold
of him and bring him out to the elders of his
town at the gate of that place. They shall say
to the elders of his town, "This son of ours is
stubborn and rebellious. He will not obey us.
He is a glutton and a drunkard." Then all the
men of the town shall stone him to death. So
you shall purge the evil from your midst; and
all Israel will hear, and be afraid.
(Deuteronomy 21:18–21)

Philip Greven, in commenting on this passage, points
out that the price of filial disobedience is death. Moses'
injunctions clearly mirrored the will of Yahweh, who
often killed those he judged to be disobedient or rebellious. Chastisements, in the form of physical pun-
ishments with the rod, were often only the first stage
in the progression of discipline from pain to death.[6]
If Yahweh orders death to those who defy their parents, what right has a court of law to interfere in the
religious training of rebellious children?

Just recently, I spent two weeks with five other
men who along with me were taking part in a phar-
maceutical study. One day, at lunch, a member of
our group was telling about his experience doing obedience training for German shepherd dogs. He said

to us, "If you want to teach a dog to lie down, you have to be willing to do something that appears to be painful to the dog and to do it forcefully the first time. You take hold of the dog's choke collar, get the dog's attention by calling his name and saying, 'Sit!' Then jerk in a downward motion as hard as you can on the choke collar. This will pull the startled dog down to the ground with such force that he will from then on respond immediately to the command to 'lie.'"

I found this advice on how to train dogs harsh, but I found the response of two of the men in our group to be unthinkable. They said almost immediately, "Say, that could also apply to child rearing." They went on to argue that it was the responsibility of parents to break the will of the child, much as you might break the will of a dog, in order to instill good behavior and obedience. I knew that both of these men were raised in the church (one the son of a Lutheran minister, the other raised in a deeply religious Roman Catholic family and educated in Catholic schools all of his life) and I was sickened to have confirmed what I had been reading on the religious roots of child abuse. It was interesting to note that the two men who joined me in objecting to the analogy were the two in our group who were no longer active in the Christian church.

Child abuse, in some cases, is directly attributable to what parents have been taught by a distorted Christian religion. And that abuse is not always physical. In many cases it is mental or emotional. Donald Capps is the William Harte Felmeth Professor of Pastoral Theology at Princeton Theological Seminary. In 1992, he wrote an article for the *Journal for the Scientific Study of Religion* which he titled "Religion and Child Abuse: Perfect Together." In that article, he tells about asking a group of people to recall any experiences they had had as children in which a religious idea had caused them mental suffering. Given time, each member of the group remembered an instance in which a religious idea, taught by a well-intentioned adult, caused that person unnecessary mental or emotional anguish. Instances reported included one person who believed that she had committed "the unpardonable sin." However, she wasn't sure that she had, because she never could figure out exactly what it was. Another person was frightened by the injunction at the Communion service not to drink of Christ's blood or eat of his body unworthily, because, once again, there was no explanation as to what constituted unworthiness when approaching the Lord's table. Still another person recalled being assured by a church school teacher that if he had enough faith his prayers would be answered. You can imagine how this young boy felt after praying for healing for an aunt who had cancer only to see her die from this dread disease. He was devastated because he felt that he had prayed with all the faith he had. He said to Capps, "The life went out of my faith at that point, and it has taken all these years to get this much of it back." Commenting on this last man's experience, Capps writes, "In concert with Carl Goldberg's (1993) argument that shame always involves a sense of incompetence, I believe this boy's inability to save his aunt through prayer was a shaming experience, the proof of his incompetence, and that shame, along with fear, are the most common experiences of torment caused by religious ideas."[7]

Adults have told me similar stories of childhood experiences with religious teachings which, rather than bringing solace and comfort, brought turmoil and confusion. I am convinced that Capps is right when he theorizes that false or misleading religious teaching can be as abusive as physical punishment for children. Mental and emotional suffering can be as painful and as destructive as physical violence and when we encourage people to talk about their own experiences of abusive religious teaching, the magnitude and severity of the problem will come to light.

The appalling thing about religious child abuse is that it is so often the result of misguided leaders who hold up certain biblical passages as proof texts, while ignoring other texts and the clear teaching of the Bible as a whole. No one can deny that there are biblical texts, such as the Deuteronomy passage quoted earlier, which counsel corporal punishment as the means for bending children to the will of their parents and, ostensibly, the will of God. Several passages in the

Book of Proverbs can be cited to prove that God expects us to use severe physical discipline to remold the corrupt nature of the child into something more acceptable to God. Undoubtedly, the most familiar admonition in this regard is the one which says,

> Do not withhold discipline from
>   your children;
> if you beat them with a rod,
>   they will not die.
> If you beat them with the rod,
>   you will save their lives from Sheol.
>   (Proverbs 23:13–14)

Several other passages in the Old Testament and a few in the New Testament picture God as a stern ruler who brooks no disobedience and who calls upon parents to instill discipline in their children, using whatever violent measures are necessary.

We cannot deny that these passages exist. However, there are other passages that point to God *as a loving parent who withholds punishment* even for those who deserve it, and who constantly seeks to win back the love of those who are alienated from their Creator, not by threat of punishment and the crushing of our will, but by the gentle persuasion of love. There are passages in both the Old and New Testaments that represent another stream of teaching: namely, that the basic nature of all human life, but especially

that of children, is not evil, but tends toward goodness. How else can we interpret the divine assessment
of the whole creation in the Book of Genesis? The
writer of the first chapter of Genesis pictures a God
who pauses after each act of creation to evaluate what
has been made, and who concludes with great satis-
faction, "God saw everything that he had made, and
indeed, it was very good" (Genesis 1:31). That assessment obviously includes human beings, who stand
at the pinnacle of creation, who are made in God's
image, who bear the very likeness of their Creator.

The Psalmist echoes the words of Genesis:

> When I look at your heavens,
>   the work of your fingers,
> the moon and the stars that
>   you have established;
> what are human beings that you
>   are mindful of them,
> mortals that you care for them?
>
> Yet you have made them a little
>   lower than God,
> and crowned them with glory
>   and honor.
> You have given them dominion
>   over the works of your hands;
> you have put all things under
>   their feet,

all sheep and oxen,
    and also the beasts of the field,
the birds of the air, and the fish
    of the sea,
whatever passes along the
    paths of the seas. (Psalm 8:3–8)

As we see Jesus take little children gently into his arms, we glimpse this other picture of God and of ourselves. Jesus, in response to his disciples' question about who is the greatest in the kingdom of heaven, calls a child into their midst. He said, "Truly I tell you, unless you change and become like children, you will never enter the kingdom of heaven. Whoever becomes humble like this child is the greatest in the kingdom of heaven. Whoever welcomes one such child in my name welcomes me" (Matthew 18:3–5). Then, Jesus continues: "If any of you put a stumbling block before one of these little ones who believe in me, it would be better for you if a great millstone were fastened around your neck and you were drowned in the depth of the sea" (Matthew 18:6).

From these and many other similar passages, and from the central emphasis of scripture, Phil Quinn draws the following conclusion:

The goal of parenting, then, is not to change children, to transform them from evil to good,

but to make them more of what they already
are – inherently good.

Instead of beating the devil out of children
in order to break their rebellious spirits and
thereby save their souls, the call to parenting
from this perspective is a call to stewardship.
We are shepherds placed in charge of God's
own sheep – his [sic] children. It is our duty to
nurture the spirit, not break it; to protect the
body, not strike it; to be good stewards of what
God has placed in our care.[8]

Can the church teach this kind of parenting and model
this kind of love so that abuse of children can be diminished? Most definitely! In fact, it already does teach
and live out of this model whenever it demonstrates in
its life that children are welcome, that they are loved
and treasured just as they are. When children are wel-
comed into worship and made to feel a part of the
worshipping community, when pastors and worship
committees incorporate into worship services elements
which children can appreciate and understand, when
children are not expected to be little adults but are
allowed to exercise their muscles and lungs in appropriate ways, when adults speak to children and welcome them with open arms and open hearts, when
children are accepted as valued members from whom
adults can learn, when the church is a place where
children feel safe and secure, then the church is mod-

eling the kind of love and respect which parents can emulate in their daily life with their children.

As I conclude this chapter, I feel like Donald Capps did as he ended the article which I referred to earlier. He realized, he said, that he had mounted a strong attack, perhaps bordering on tirade, against religion, and yet he hoped that he would not be viewed as an opponent of Christianity. So he wanted to conclude on a different note and his conclusion is one which I share. He comes back to the point which I made at the beginning of this book – religion is, at various times, an agent of great blessings, and an agent of great curse. It gives us wings to fly away from the destructive abuse of children and it contains a weight of negative teachings about human nature which drags us back down into that sin.

Capps ends by recalling the man who was unable, as a child, to save his aunt through prayer. This same man told another story about another teacher. This teacher would read stories to the children allowing them to take turns sitting on her lap while she did so. As the man spoke of this, his eyes filled with tears – something deep inside him had been touched by the love of this woman. Capps then says, "If only we could forgo the lofty pretensions of religion, those that cause us to torture and torment the children, and instead tell simple stories of human goodness, courage, resourcefulness, cooperation, and above all, of loving and being loved..."[9]

Inherent in this conclusion is the key by which religion moves away from abuse and in the direction of that which is life-giving and affirming. We never make it all the way, but we can take great strides as we sort through our experiences as children and determine to accentuate those that taught us how to love and be loved, and to eliminate, as far as possible, those which caused us pain and suffering.

5

RELIGION
AND ABUSE
OF WOMEN

For me, as a male, to talk about the abuse of women is obviously presumptuous. I do so fully aware of my limitations and the secondhand nature of my accounts. Nonetheless, I approach this subject with great concern because of the trauma that I have witnessed in the lives of those women who have come to me desperately seeking help from intolerably abusive situations. I have seen their determination and courage as they dared to do something about their abuse, even though they were unsure how they would support themselves and their children. I have also counseled women whose desperation was evident as they realized that they did not have the emotional strength or financial ability to leave an abusive husband.

I have witnessed the trauma of physical, verbal, and emotional abuse of women in the congregations I have served and I have often felt sad and helpless. At the same time, female clergy and counselors have helped me recognize other forms of abuse that they suffer – forms of abuse which may not be life threatening, but which are terribly damaging nonetheless. Finally, I have become very much aware that when a society and a religion devalue women, they rob everyone, males included, of the possibility of wholeness and health. That is a tragedy for all and men should be as concerned as women about this issue.

The world has been dominated and controlled by men for many centuries and the havoc and destruction of that domination is well documented. For thousands of years women have been thought of and treated essentially like cattle, or some other possession. Women have had very few rights except for those given by male leaders or guardians. The first-born *male* inherited the family estate, even when he wasn't the first-born *child*. Women could not own property; they could not vote; they were required to be submissive to their husbands; they did not have equal protection under the law. A family felt blessed with the birth of a male child; but female children were often unwanted and in some cases killed. The list of deprivations which women have suffered is endless. In society and in religion, women have been considered second-class citizens, or worse. They certainly haven't been seen as fully human and as valuable as men. Some would argue that this is what God intended.

Fortunately, society and to a lesser degree religion are beginning to see that this is *not* what God intended; and changes in the status and affirmation of women are coming about at an ever accelerating rate. We still have a long, long way to go before the equal partnership between men and women, which God intended, is realized. But over the last 50 years we have finally begun to move in that direction.

Unfortunately, one of the greatest hindrances to that movement has been and still is found in religion. Patriarchy is alive and well in most religious circles and it has resisted change every step of the way. Furthermore, it will *continue* to resist change as long as God is believed to be a male deity, revealed most fully by a male savior, served by an exclusively male priesthood. As long as our language about God perpetuates an exclusively male image, as long as we continue to use words like "mankind" instead of "humanity" to refer to God's people, as long as our concept of power in the church is concerned with the right to dominate rather than to nurture, we make it impossible for women to inherit fully their God-given status as children of God, equal in every way to men.

Let me share with you one woman's experience which speaks so forcefully to the point. Writing in *Church and Society*, Jenny Miller describes an incident which took place while she was a student at a Presbyterian seminary – an incident which changed the course of her life and work. It was the first Sunday in Advent and Jenny was reading the creation story from Genesis 1 and 2 to her four-year-old daughter and her six-year-old son. When she came to the passage which talked about people being created in God's image, it occurred to Jenny that this concept might be hard for a four- and six-year-old to grasp, so she asked her children if they knew what that phrase meant. She went on to explain that it means that we are all made to be like God.

Her daughter's response astonished Jenny. She said, *"Mommy! Mommy, I'm not like God! I'm a girl."* Jenny describes what followed and her own reaction:

Explaining as I might, I could not budge either my four-year-old daughter or my six-year-old son from their acceptance of the idea, *received from the church* [emphasis mine], that God is male, nor could I dislodge its corollary, that the brother is God-like while the sister is not. Everybody knows, Mom, they persisted, that God is a boy. And even as my sturdy daughter defended her position I could hear in her words, I'm not like…I'm not like…the beginnings of confusion, the genesis of grief. My beautiful daughter! Four years old, theologically informed, already clued in to the message that she is not-like, a less-than, to men and to God.[1]

What was most shocking to Jenny was the realization that the church was the origin, the instructor, in this false image of God. She continues her account:

The children, as leery of inclusive language as many adults I know, went to bed unconverted and somewhat bemused by my strange ideas. I stayed awake, badly shaken by *the distortion that Christian education and worship had been introducing into my children's lives* [emphasis mine]. The two of them were entirely willing to concede that my son was something – in God's image – that my daughter was not. *In faithfully attending church and Sunday school* [emphasis mine] my children were inadvertently being given, receiving, and owning not only a misleading notion of God but, what was worse to me, a dangerous, deep, and false distinction between them: a perception of male is-ness and female is-not-ness that was a distortion of the true humanity of both of them.

Too often, the church persists in teaching a concept of God that is woefully inadequate. God is not male or female – God is Spirit totally beyond our comprehension. We use anthropomorphic language to describe God because we have no other way of talking about the creator of all things. As Christians, we believe that God is personal in the sense that God can respond to our feelings and enter into a deeply personal relationship. But, having said that, we must admit that God remains a mystery. God cannot be captured in either our concept of maleness or femaleness. The most we can say is that in God dwell all the best attributes we ascribe to both men and women. The Bible pictures God in a variety of ways – as Lord, father, spirit, mother hen or eagle, creator, comforter, etc. No one of these images, nor all of them together, can capture the essence of what God is, and we are guilty of the gravest sin, the sin of idolatry, when we claim to know otherwise.

In her book *Beyond God the Father,* Mary Daly challenges us to be aware of the images which stand behind our names for God and to be willing to look for new ways to describe our encounter with divine reality. She says, "Part of the challenge is to recognize the poverty of all words and symbols and the fact of our past idolatry regarding them, and then to turn to our own resources for bringing about the radically new in our own lives."[2] Theologians, including many feminist theologians, are attempting to do just that. They are seeking to find ways to talk about God which do not perpetuate images of patriarchy – of male domination and control. Mary Daly suggests one such way when she asks, "Why indeed must God be a noun? Why not a verb – the most active and dynamic of all? Hasn't the naming of God as a noun been an act of murdering that dynamic verb? And isn't the verb infinitely more personal than a mere static noun? The anthropomorphic symbols for God may be intended to convey personality, but they fail to convey that God is Be-ing."[3]

What I hear Daly saying is that as long as we think of God as a noun we will automatically return to an anthropomorphic picture in our mind. And because of long conditioning, that picture probably will be one of a male deity, sitting upon a judgment throne, waiting to pass sentence on those with whom *he* is displeased.

We need, then, to rediscover the answer which God gave to Moses when Moses asked for God's name. In the encounter with God at the burning bush, God responds to Moses by saying, "Thus you shall say to the Israelites, '*I Am* has sent me to you'" (Exodus 3:14). God cannot be put in a box. God defies our best efforts to describe what God is. God is dynamic. God is as much a verb as a noun.

Because we get our images of God from the church, each religious community must wrestle with new ways of talking about God which challenge the patriarchy of thousands of years, and which open for us an understanding of God that validates and celebrates the worth and value of women as well as men. Equally important, the church must take a new look at how it interprets scripture and at how it understands those passages which have been used to support patriarchy – the conviction that God ordained a hierarchy in which men are given more worth and value than women and are expected to rule over and dominate them. Abuse of women could be significantly diminished if Christian leaders and lay people were to look again at the Bible and discover what God actually intended for men and women.

That investigation must begin at the beginning, with pivotal texts in the first three chapters of Genesis, the first book of the Bible. According to the biblical account, God crowned creation by bringing into being *both* men and women. The long-standing translation of verse 26 of the first chapter of Genesis is misleading. For all of our lives, we have heard, "Then God said, 'Let us make man in our image.'" What that verse actually says is reflected in the New Revised Standard Version of the Bible, where it is rendered, "Then God said, 'Let us make humankind in our image.'" There is no doubt that this is the intent if we look at the next verse, verse 27, which says, "So God created humankind in God's image, in the image of God, God created them; *male and female* God created them."

However, when we turn to the third chapter of Genesis, we find a text which seemingly seals the fate of women as subordinate to men by God's design. It pictures God as saying to the first woman, Eve, "Your desire shall be for your husband, and he shall rule over you" (Genesis 3:16). That would seem to leave no doubt as to the dominant role which men are intended to play, except for the fact that what we have pictured here is not God's *intention*, but rather the *consequences* of human mistrust and our rebellion against our Creator. The third chapter of Genesis is a parable that was told by an inspired storyteller to help us understand what went wrong with God's good creation, and what the consequences are of human disobedience and pride. It does not tell us, then, what God *intended*. Rather, it shows us the twisted and perverted shape of things which human beings have brought upon themselves.

We can be grateful to women theologians who are beginning to open our eyes to an understanding of scripture which has eluded male theologians for centuries. Johanna W. H. van Wijk-Bos is one of these theologians. The interpretation of Genesis 3 which I offered above comes, in fact, from her book *Reformed and Feminist* and her summary of the work of her colleagues Phyllis Byrd and Phyllis Trible, both Old Testament scholars.[4]

In commenting further on the fact that the words of Genesis 3 are descriptive of what life is like as a result of our mistrust and rebellion from God, rather than *prescriptive*, Wijk-Bos says the following:

The complementing contrast to this text is Galatians 3:28: "There is neither Jew nor Greek, there is neither slave nor free, there is neither male nor female, for you are all one in Christ Jesus" (RSV). Here the new creation is announced as a fulfillment of what the creation was intended to be.[5]

The question with which the church and each individual Christian must wrestle is, "What is God's intention – male domination, or mutuality between male and female?" It is a crucial question, especially for the issue of the abuse of women, but also for the abuse of children, minorities, and nature as well. No one takes *all* of the Bible literally, but those who take *selected* passages of scripture literally will find it difficult to accept new insights from God's word. At the same time, those who are willing to let the Spirit of God provide new insights into what is revealed in scripture, will find the results to be quite surprising and liberating. This is the challenge which Johanna Wijk-Bos makes when she reminds us:

As in the days of the Reformation, the Bible may point to a need for a radical reformation of what has become misformed in the church. The authority of the Bible may prevent the faithful from worshiping an institution, even a Reformed institution. Also, by their emphasis on the Bible, the Reformers did not intend to put a book in the center of belief and practice. Rather, they intended to focus belief and practice on God...If the Bible is the living Word of God, it might be as surprising and unmanageable as God.[6]

It was this unmanageable God who broke through stereotypes in Jesus Christ giving us a new understanding of the relationship between male and female. In a culture and a religious tradition which was deeply androcentric and patriarchal, Jesus dared to incorporate women in his movement in a way which called into question the assumption that God had ordained women to be second-class persons. Marcus Borg, in his book *Meeting Jesus Again for the First Time*, says:

The role of women in the Jesus movement is striking. The stories of Jesus' interaction with women are remarkable. They range from his defense of the woman who outraged an all-male banquet not only by entering it but also by (unveiled and with hair unbraided) washing his feet with her hair, to his being hosted by Mary and Martha and affirming Mary's role as disciple, to his learning from a Syro-Phoencian Gentile woman. Women were apparently part of the itinerant group traveling with Jesus. Indeed, they were apparently among his most devoted followers, as the stories of their presence at his death suggests. The movement itself was financially supported by some wealthy women. Moreover, the evidence is compelling that women played leadership roles in the Post-Easter community.[7]

If Jesus is the reflection of God on this earth, as Christians have claimed, it is time for us to take seriously how he challenged the prevailing understanding of the role and place of women in society and in religion. Jesus takes us back to God's original design where men and women were created as equals and he calls us to move beyond the curse of male dominance so that we may live in a redeemed community where men and women work together as partners to create a better world for all. To get back to what God intended will demand a radical break with long-held ideas and teachings of the church, but it holds the promise of a great liberation for both males and females as we discover again the original intention of God in the story of creation. When we follow Jesus' lead in redefining the role of women in the eyes of our distorted culture and theology, we will have removed one of the underlying causes of the abuse of women and will have laid the foundation for religion becoming a positive force in the struggle for change.

6

THE ULTIMATE
FORM OF ABUSE

Religious abuse is widespread and it comes in many different forms. In most cases, it affects the life of one individual bringing misery and suffering, either mental or physical, to that person. One form of abuse exists, however, which I consider to be the ultimate abuse. This form of abuse is particularly dangerous because it has the potential to destroy not only individuals, but also to alienate whole groups of people, plunging them into great conflicts which lead to much death and destruction.

I am speaking of the abuse of *exclusivity* – the conviction that one's belief system is the only correct or valid one, and, therefore, that the tenets of those who hold different understandings of God are not only wrong, but dangerous and must be destroyed because they pose a threat to the souls of those who might be led astray. Exclusivity, when followed to its logical conclusion, must lead to the attempt to eliminate false teachers because those who believe they have the only valid understanding of God must protect others from the eternal punishment which awaits all who might be influenced by these false teachers.

Actually, those who would destroy others who believe differently from themselves are acting upon what they perceive to be the highest motives. They want to prevent people from being contaminated with false doctrines which could endanger their souls. Therefore, they feel it necessary either to convert these false teachers or to silence them in some fashion, even if this means death.

John Calvin, the father of the Presbyterian Church, was acting out of a concern for others who might be led astray by the teachings of Michael Servitus when he consented to having the man put to death by the rulers in Geneva, Switzerland. Servitus' greatest crime was that he took the teachings of the Reformation too seriously. He really believed that people were free to interpret the Bible as they understood it and to share their understandings of God with others. Servitus did not believe in the Trinity as the church had defined this doctrine. Calvin believed that Servitus' departures from the official teachings of the church were serious enough to pose a threat to the salvation of those who might be influenced by his interpretation of scripture.

Actually, the death of Jesus Christ was the result of similar reasoning. The religious leaders of Jesus' day felt threatened by this itinerant preacher who spoke with the authority of God and who challenged their interpretation of scripture and their understanding of how one entered into a right relationship with God. The Pharisees and Scribes thought they knew what one must do to be acceptable to God. They believed that Jesus was leading people away from God when he taught that blind and loveless obedience to "the law" could actually stand in the way of a person's relationship with God. Jesus taught that all the law could be summed up in two brief commands: "Love the Lord your God with all your heart, and with all your soul, and with all your mind…You shall love your neighbor as yourself" (Matthew 22:37–39). The religious leaders who heard this feared that the common people would become followers of the Galilean and would neglect the details of the law which must be kept in order to retain God's favor upon the Jews and usher in the messianic kingdom. So they plotted and eventually brought about Jesus' death.

In retrospect, we marvel at how religious men could have a man killed whose only crime was that he preached about love of God and neighbor, but we must remember that that was not at all how they saw the matter. They believed that there was only *one* way to please God and that way was through meticulous observance of the letter of the law. They believed that what Jesus was teaching was a threat not only to an individual's relationship with God, but also to the survival of the Jewish nation and any future glory which God had promised the chosen people. Therefore, they thought they had no alternative but to silence him.

Unfortunately, they did not have the advice of the wisest among their own number, who counseled a different approach. When the disciples of Jesus were arrested for carrying on his teaching after his death, a respected teacher among the Pharisees by the name of Gamaliel warned against a similar silencing of Jesus' followers. He said to the council, "Fellow Israelites, consider carefully what you propose to do to these men…I tell you, keep away from these men and let them alone; because if this plan or this undertaking is of human origin, it will fail; but if it is of God, you will not be able to overthrow them – in that case you may even be found fighting against God!" (Acts 5:35–39).

Most of us can see the wisdom of that advice as we look back upon the death of Jesus and the persecution of his followers. Unfortunately, many religious leaders and teachers find it hard to take that advice when it comes to their own understanding of the truth and they look for ways to silence those who disagree with them. Most of the conflicts around the world today are motivated and continued, at least in part, by an element of religious exclusivity, just as they have been across the ages. Separating religious, political, and economic reasons for bloodshed is often quite difficult. But there is no disputing the fact that religion plays a large part in fostering strife among groups of people who are each convinced that they are doing the will of God when they destroy those who teach a different concept of God.

Hans Küng, the great Roman Catholic theologian, speaks to this point when he says, "I became increasingly aware that discussion with the other world religions is actually essential for survival, necessary for the sake of peace in the world. Are not the most fanatical and cruel political struggles colored, inspired, and legitimized by religion?"[1] Küng concludes: "Peace among the religions is the prerequisite for peace among the nations."[2]

All religions have at the core of their teaching a central ethic of love and harmony. Yet despite their own teachings which call for a peaceful settlement of disputes, we discover that religions are often the fomenters of strife and bloodshed. Some of this conflict which has its origin in religion can be traced to the ambitions of selfish religious leaders. But much of it finds its origin in an exclusivity which sees other religions as the enemy to be destroyed in order to maintain the purity of the one true faith. The Crusades of the 12th and 13th centuries, the Inquisition which existed from 303 CE to 1834 CE to root out heresy in the Roman Catholic Church, and numerous religious wars throughout Europe, found their justification in the exclusive claims of each group of Christians. And this exclusivity is at least in part responsible for current conflicts in the Middle East between Christians, Jews, and Muslims; in Southeast Asia between Hindus, Buddhists, and Sikhs; in Africa between traditional African tribes. With the revival of fundamentalism in all the major religions of the world, exclusivity poses an especially grave threat to peace in the world today.

Exclusivity leads to bloodshed on a grand scale and it also separates families and friends. I remember vividly a couple who joined our church. The husband came from a Presbyterian background while his wife had been raised in the Church of Christ. The couple found in our congregation support not only for themselves but also for their four children, two of whom were adopted black children. However, the wife's parents felt so strongly about her leaving the Church of Christ that they cut off all relationship with her and the children. Essentially, the parents disowned their own daughter and grandchildren because they felt that she had been led astray by a false religion and was endangering not only her own soul but the souls of her children as well.

Some may have a hard time believing that people who are followers of Jesus Christ could feel so strongly that others who belong to another branch of Christianity are going to hell. But the evidence of this exclusivity is everywhere. For centuries the Roman Catholic Church taught that there was no salvation outside of it. The Roman dogma *Extra ecclesiam nulla salus* (Outside the church, no salvation) was only recently rescinded. Listen to radio evangelists today and you will hear many claiming to have the only way to salvation, not only for those outside the Christian faith, but also for those who already consider themselves Christian. Exclusivity is alive and active and the only thing that prevents witch hunts and the burning of heretics today is a separation of civil and ecclesiastical power. You can understand, then, why Terry Muck, Associate Professor of Comparative Religions at Austin Presbyterian Seminary, would rephrase Küng to read, "There will be no peace among the religions of the world until there is peace among the Christians of the world."[3]

Peace in our world will not be possible until the Christian religion and the other world religions rediscover the central teaching of their great spiritual leaders and their sacred writings – a central teaching which calls us into a new relationship of trust with a God whom we call by many names and into a new relationship of love and justice with all the peoples of the earth. Peace in our world will wait until we break out of our culturally conditioned and provincial belief systems, until we learn from each other's religious experiences to recognize the rich and diverse tapestry of God's interaction with human beings across the centuries. Peace in the world will be postponed until we lay down our swords and stop trying to force our belief system on others; until we begin, instead, to change by the gentle persuasion of love those in every religion who still believe that theirs is the only true path which leads to God and to salvation.

John Hick describes his conversion to a more universal understanding of God's interaction with humankind in his book *God Has Many Names.* As he wrestled with Christian exclusivity, he tells of a turning point in his life:

A move at that time to Birmingham, England, with its large Muslim, Sikh, and Hindu communities, as well as its older Jewish community, made this problem a live and immediate one. For I was drawn into the work which is variously called race relations and community relations, and soon had friends and colleagues in all these non-Christian religious communities as well as in the large black community from the Caribbean. And occasionally attending worship in mosque and synagogue, temple and gurdwara, it was evident to me that essentially the same kind of thing is taking place in them as in a Christian church – namely, human beings opening their minds to a higher divine Reality, known as personal and good and as demanding righteousness and love between man and man [*sic*]...Without ever being tempted to become either a Hindu or a Buddhist I could see that within these ancient traditions men and women are savingly related to the eternal Reality from which we all live.[4]

Peace in the world, in our families, in our neighborhoods, and in our hearts will be an elusive dream until we deal with this matter of exclusivity in our own thinking. Exclusivity is the greatest enemy of grace. Those who preach and teach that there is only one way to God are substituting works and dogma and the traditions of human beings for the grace of God, which blows where it wills and enters our lives in a variety of ways.

7

THE ABUSE
OF CLERGY

As I have talked about the abuses of religion, I may have given the impression that clergy are the chief perpetrators of that abuse. In some cases that is true. Certainly Jesus' encounters with the priests of his day show us how religious leaders can be inflexible and blind to new truth when it confronts and challenges their long-held beliefs. Like the prophets of the Old Testament, Jesus discovered that these religious leaders did not look kindly upon those who pointed out their hypocrisy or challenged their authority or threatened their livelihood. There can be little doubt that clergy are a part of the problem of religious abuse.

However, there is another side to this coin, which must not be overlooked. Clergy, themselves, are often the recipients of religious abuse. That abuse comes in many forms and this examination would be incomplete without exposing as many of them as possible.

Recently I met a friend from high school days. I lost contact with John after we left high school but I knew that he had entered the ministry in the Southern Baptist Church. Then a man who had coached both of us in track wrote to tell me that he had heard John preach at a revival many years ago and that John was a powerful speaker. When I saw John a couple of months ago, he was a security guard at a large retirement complex. I asked him where he was preaching. He said he was looking for a church. Then he added, "It used to be that you were called to tell people the good news of God's love in Jesus Christ. Now you are called to be a referee between opposing factions in the church. Often, you get caught in the middle and attacked by both sides."

Unfortunately, John's experience is not unique. Many pastors find that a good portion of their energy and time is spent putting out fires of discontent in their congregations. And, at times, they get "burned" in their efforts to be peacemakers.

In the great majority of cases of discontent, the issue is not a matter of theological or doctrinal importance. More often than not, the dispute is over what color carpet to put in the parlor, or the kind of music the new choir director has chosen, or what time the morning service will begin. The church is a large family and like all families it has its squabbles. The trouble is that the pastor often becomes the focal point of the family feud and ends up the target of the wrath of both sides of the quarrel. The introduction of courses in conflict management in mainline seminaries is testimony to this problem which many ministers, priests, and rabbis will encounter in their communities.

It should not surprise us that conflict is present in every church family to one degree or another. Conflict has been a part of every major world religion. It is present in the Hindu, Islamic, Buddhist, and Jewish religions, and it has been present in the Christian faith from its very beginning. Conflict is also present in secular businesses and offices, in academic communities, in every level of government. Wherever human beings gather to work together, people will have to deal with conflict.

So what is unique about conflict in the Christian community? Let me suggest a few things that make it different from conflict in other situations.

G. Lloyd Rediger has written a book, *Clergy Killers*, which has received a lot of attention since its publication in 1997. In his book, Rediger defines clergy killers as "people who intentionally target pastors for serious injury or destruction."[1] He differentiates clergy killers from others in the congregation who may disagree with the pastor or oppose some project that the pastor has suggested. The distinguishing mark of the clergy killer is an evil intent to do harm to the pastor by whatever means are available or necessary. Rediger, like Scott Peck in his book *People of the Lie*, believes that there are evil people in this world whose lives are controlled by a demonic force working within them. And he believes that some of these people are present in congregations.

As I talk with church executives, seminary professors, and pastoral counselors, I find that most of them feel that Rediger's book is worthy of consideration. It is used in some seminaries in courses dealing with conflict in the church. When I expressed my own reservation about the idea of people possessed by an evil spirit, a friend in the ministry, who has worked on conflicted situations in several churches, told me about three cases he had observed where it seemed to him that people had been driven to evil acts that were beyond the ordinary. It is perhaps natural that evil within the church gets magnified, because the intent to destroy the ministry of a pastor strikes not just at the individual, but at God, whom the church seeks, however imperfectly, to worship and serve.

Rediger's book needs to be taken seriously for another reason. His chapter on "collateral damage" makes us aware of the fact that clergy abuse goes beyond the pastor. We are familiar with the term "collateral damage" from its use in military operations where it refers to damage which goes beyond the military target to include civilian casualties. Rediger uses the term to refer to the spouse, children, and close friends who are wounded when the pastor is attacked by members of the congregation.

The expectations placed on clergy spouses and family are far above those placed on family members of people in other professions. I have never met my doctor's wife or my lawyer's husband and really do not care what type of people they are. I certainly do not demand that their spouses be knowledgeable in the fields of medicine or law. Even if I knew my doctor's spouse, I would not be concerned if she wore short skirts or too much make-up. That really is none of my business, nor would I be concerned that her personal choices affected the competency of my doctor. However, everyone in the church knows the pastor's spouse. If the spouse is a woman, she is often expected to be an expert Bible teacher, to lead in prayer public, to attend women's circle meetings, and to arrange for meals for the sick. In other words, she is a *partner* in her husband's ministry, and, as such, she can be praised for her expertise and faithfulness or she can be criticized and attacked, especially by those who do not like her husband. When the pastor is out of favor with certain members of the congregation, finding fault with a spouse is an excellent way to attack.

And it is not only the pastor's spouse who experiences abuse from the congregation. Recently, I asked a presbytery executive for examples of collateral damage which she had observed in her work. She gave me an example of abuse which came from her own experience as part of a pastor's family. The story she sent to me was not about abuse which she had suffered, but rather about abuse that was directed at her daughter. This is that she wrote:

Our daughter, Sarah, is adopted and the congregation my husband was serving knew that. When she was about 10 years old, she loved to bring friends with her to church. In one of the remodelings of the sanctuary, the position of the chancel and the pews had been reversed. The result was that there were two small balconies now in the back of the church. One had no access, but the other had a narrow staircase behind a small door. All the children liked to climb up there on occasion.

One Sunday, Sarah had a friend at church and they asked if they could sit in the little balcony. I reminded them that if they made noise or "carried on" it would be distracting to Dad – and that MOM would be watching them! They promised to be good and did very well. When they came down the stairs, they were greeted by one of the older women in the church, who said to them, "You know that is no place for you to be during church. *You're going to have to be very careful that you don't turn out to be a bad person like your real mother."*

As I read that account, I was almost convinced that some people *are* possessed by an evil spirit, because I find it difficult to explain this woman's cruelty and hurtful words to this young girl in any other way. Maybe this is what we mean when we say that people are "mean spirited."

Rediger has done a good job of alerting us to various forms of clergy abuse. However, there are other unique features of clergy abuse which must also be considered. The role of the pastor, for instance, is different from any other form of leadership in some very important ways. For instance, clergy are called to be both *pastor/priest* and *prophet* to the congregation. The pastor/priestly role includes comforting those who are ill or troubled, leading worship, administering the sacraments, as well as marrying and burying members of the congregation.

It might seem that this particular role of the clergy would bring little conflict. However, that is not always the case. During our last year in seminary, we were warned repeatedly by the faculty not to change anything in the order of worship for at least a year after we had arrived at our first parish. People in the church, as in most other places, do not take kindly to change, but especially not to change in the order of worship. In more liturgical churches this may not be as great an issue, but there are "sacred cows" in every congregation which must not be disturbed too soon after the arrival of a new pastor.

In that same vein, the pastor/priest will find that people will draw comparisons with his or her predecessor. If the former pastor preached from a manuscript and the new pastor delivers the sermon in a more informal fashion, there may be trouble. If the former pastor had an "open door policy" to his or her office, the new pastor may experience criticism if the office door is frequently closed. If the former minister put emphasis on visitation while the new minister spends more time on study and sermon preparation, people may feel uncared for.

There are many ways that the priestly/pastor role can prove hazardous to clergy, but the role of the prophet has even more potential for angry reaction. The prophet speaks for God and the pastor must interpret the will of God for the people as she or he finds it in scripture. This can mean calling into question the actions of those who fail to demonstrate compassion and concern for those who are less fortunate. It can also mean challenging those who are rich to share their wealth and power with those who are poor and powerless.

When the prophet dares to speak on social issues, he or she will often encounter the same kind of anger that prophets have faced in every religion, in every place, in every time. People feel strongly about a whole array of issues. Pastors who challenge long-held positions, attitudes, or prejudices can find themselves in deep conflict with those who feel that they are being attacked.

A friend and colleague in the ministry discovered the price the prophet must pay in the first church he served after graduating from seminary – a rural congregation in Virginia in the early 1970s. My friend made it clear in sermons and in conversations that he believed that biblical faith would not support segregation and that therefore, the people of this community and this church should support integration. He immediately felt the hostility of his congregation and the community. One of his few friends in the church warned him that he and his wife should get out of the area as soon as possible. So, late at night, they threw what possessions they could in their car and fled before an angry mob arrived.

When the prophet becomes concrete and specific, pointing out a social attitude or action that God deplores, in the eyes of many he or she has "stopped preaching and started meddling." Today the issue is not segregation, but it could be race relations, the rights of homosexuals, gun control, abortion rights, the gender gap in wages, minimum wage and livable wage, what constitutes a just war or military action, stewardship of the earth – the list could go on and on. The prophet has the potential to touch a nerve in individuals and communities, to stir up emotions and anger which are then directed back at the prophet. This dual role of pastor/priest and prophet has, as far as I know, no parallel in business or any other form of leadership.

There is another unique feature about the role of the clergy. The clergyperson is both the *servant* of the congregation and also its *shepherd*. As a servant of the congregation, the pastor is expected to be available to its members 24 hours a day. Clergy ordinarily work 50- to 60-hour weeks, with weekends filled with worship services, weddings, retreats, and many other activities. In a very real sense, a pastor's week is quite different from the ordinary. Most people say, "TGIF" (Thank God it's Friday). The pastor is more likely to say, "Oh my God, it's Friday and the sermon isn't finished."

My son once came to me and said, "Dad, do I have to go to church every Sunday?" Fortunately, I dug deeper at what was bothering him before replying to his question. I said, "Why are you asking?" He replied, "Well, my friends get to take trips on the weekend with their families and they don't have to go to church every Sunday. We never take weekend trips because you have to preach every Sunday." At age ten, he was well aware that a preacher's schedule is different from almost everybody else's. He also knew that Christmas and Easter were two of my busiest times and that, therefore, while others usually had some time off during these holidays, I was going to be unavailable for travel or for many other forms of special family gathering.

The constancy of the demands of serving a congregation can and often does lead to burnout in clergy. In an article on theological education which appeared in *Presbyterian Outlook*, Marcia Clark Myers, associate director for churchwide personnel services, is quoted as saying that pastors get worn down by "all of the expectations – by being expected to be the guide when you really don't know the way yourself...And being sidetracked all the time by all these fights, all the focus on sex." Then Myers adds a very telling comment: "We don't see Presbyterian ministers' children going into the ministry the way we did in previous generations." Instead, "ministers are feeling that's the worst thing their kids could do. They want to spare them the pain, so they encourage them in other directions."[2]

When you combine long hours, impossible expectations, and distractions from the main motive of ministry, you have a recipe for great discontent among clergy. Add to that woefully inadequate salaries for those serving small or medium size churches, and you can understand why there is a severe shortage of pastors and priests – a problem which is only going to get worse unless something is done. People who enter the ministry don't expect to get rich, but neither do they want to live in poverty. Many seminary trained pastors begin their ministry with a large debt which must be repaid from a meager salary. Those pastors who are married and who have children often find their salary will not meet the needs of their family and provide savings for college for their children. The servant role should not include a vow of poverty, but it often does.

Then there's the shepherding role of the pastor, which we need to put in its historical context. The term shepherd suggests that the members of a congregation are like sheep whom the pastor must guide, while they follow obediently and without question, wherever they are led. There was a time when this was an apt description of the relationship between priest and parishioners. Up until the Protestant Reformation and the invention of the printing press, the priest was the only person who could read the scriptures and so lay people had no basis on which to challenge what the priest said.

Changes in that situation began to come slowly as the Bible was translated into the language of the people and was made available to others beyond the priesthood. All of this accelerated in the 19th and 20th centuries. As lay people became more biblically literate, they gained the courage to challenge a pastor's interpretation of scripture. Since there was no longer just one source of interpretation, people began to quarrel over how to understand the biblical message and the shepherd found that his or her leadership often met opposition from the pew.

In more recent times, with the rise of biblical criticism and better tools for interpreting scripture that are taught in most seminaries, the gulf between the knowledge of a pastor and his or her congregation has once again widened. The pastor is aware that the Bible is not infallible: it contains many contradictions and inaccuracies; it is a product of its time and culture and worldview. Many of its pronouncements must be questioned in the light of modern knowledge. Many of its stories are myths which lose their ability to transmit truth when they are taken literally; much of what we know and believe about Jesus was written many years after his death and reflects the bias and agenda of the writer.

Most Christians read the Bible primarily as a devotional book, if they read it at all, and know little or nothing about biblical criticism. Many would be shocked and angry to hear the story of Adam and Eve described as an ancient story or myth. After all, much of the official understanding of Jesus' mission is based on "the Fall" when Adam and Eve disobeyed God and ate of the tree of the knowledge of good and evil. According to our most prevalent theory of the atonement, Jesus came to pay the price of humanity's sin, which was inherited from Adam. If the story of Adam and Eve is a myth, then that theory and many of our other doctrines must be reexamined – a difficult and time-consuming task for both pastor and people.

As long as this huge gap exists between what informed pastors have learned in professional schools of theology and what the average layperson knows, there is bound to be conflict when the pastor attempts to share his or her knowledge with the congregation. Many times the pastor solves the problem by adapting to the congregation's level of biblical understanding, sharing little or none of what he or she has learned in seminary.

This leads to what I believe is the worst form of abuse that clergy encounter. It is the abuse of *enforced dishonesty*. Clergy are often caught in the middle between higher judicatories or ecclesiastical authorities that demand conformity to outmoded doctrinal statements and congregations that typically are more conservative than the pastor.

Over the course of my ministry, I have worked with several seminary students who worked as interns in the church I was serving. Each of them had to write their faith statement, which would be submitted to the presbytery committee overseeing their preparation for ministry. I would always ask if I could see it. After reading it, I would ask if this was what they really believed and invariably they would respond, "No, this isn't what I believe. But this is what the committee wants to think I believe." Recently, I asked another pastor who had worked with seminary interns if my experience was unique and he confirmed that it was not. Many seminary graduates enter the ministry obliged to lie or mislead the higher judicatory that determines whether they will be ordained.

Karen Armstrong tells of a similar experience of dishonesty in her training to be a nun in the Roman Catholic Church in England. In her book *Through the Narrow Gate,* Armstrong recalls how she was assigned the task of writing an essay which would assess the quality of the evidence for the resurrection. The essay was part of a course in apologetics that attempted to explain the mysteries of the faith by means of reason. As she researched the subject, she became convinced that there was no way to prove rationally that Jesus rose from the grave. She concluded that the resurrection must be accepted as a miracle, or not accepted at all. However, because she was preparing for examinations, she wrote the paper. She recounts, "I reproduced the mental gymnastics that were expected of me, *feeling all the while a sinking loss of integrity*" [emphasis mine]. She handed in her essay and her instructor, Mother Greta, praised her work. Because she trusted that her mentor had an honest mind, Armstrong dared to share with her the question of honesty that haunted her. This is how she describes what happened. "But Mother," I said quietly, staring at her intently. "It just isn't true, what I have written, is it?" Mother Greta was silent for a moment. "No, Sister," she said flatly. "No, it isn't true, but please don't tell the other novices."[3]

Unfortunately, this kind of dishonesty continues throughout the ministry of many who serve as leaders in the church. I belong to a group that has been meeting each Monday night for five years. The group came into being when a friend whom I have known since high school asked his pastor if the church would include in its fall schedule a class which would study Marcus Borg's book *Meeting Jesus Again for the First Time*. The pastor told my friend that this book was too controversial to study in their church school. So my friend invited some other members from his church to meet on Monday nights to explore Borg's book. I was invited to join as the lone Presbyterian in the midst of 12 Lutherans. Borg opened the eyes of those lay people to an understanding of scripture and of Jesus that they had never heard in church school or from the pulpit.

When the Monday night group heard Borg say in his book, "I am aware that this is still news for some Christians, even though it has been old hat in seminaries of mainline denominations throughout this century,"[4] they asked themselves why this was the first time they were hearing many of these things, which they felt came closer to what they believed. Why had their pastor never mentioned in a sermon some of the insights into the gospels that Borg revealed? Why was he reluctant to have this book discussed in a church school class?

I don't know the answer to these questions, but I can speculate about the pastor's motives. He may have been genuinely conservative and did not agree with what he had been taught in seminary. That's a possibility. But I believe that there is another possible explanation for his reticence. Borg is a controversial scholar and a member of the "Jesus Seminar." Obviously, that would make some members uneasy. With a major building campaign coming up, unhappy members were the last thing this pastor wanted. He may have been unwilling to let his members discuss the book and decide for themselves, because that would expose the gap between his own seminary training and what he had been willing to share with his congregation.

Actually, this pastor doesn't have a choice now. Recently, Peter Jennings, the ABC News anchorman, aired a program called "The Search for Jesus," which was seen by millions of people. In that program, Jennings interviewed Borg and other scholars who presented the public with an array of different ways of looking at this man, Jesus. What was once a closed theological discussion is now a matter of public debate. Either pastors begin to share with their congregations some of the biblical insights they learned in seminary, or they will be seen to have their heads stuck in the sand. Now all pastors are in the position I found myself in when I asked a young lady from our congregation if she had taken a Bible course during her first year at a denominational college. She said that she had and then she added, "They sure don't teach

Bible the way we learned it in church school." For that young lady, there was no turning back to older views of the Bible. If she stays in the church (which is highly unlikely), she will go to a church where the pastor is honest enough and trusts his or her congregation enough to share with them the insights he or she learned in seminary.

Roman Catholic priests face a different kind of problem with honesty. In his book *Papal Sin*, Garry Wills exposes structures of deceit in papal circles that perpetuate biblically indefensible teachings. Pronouncements on clergy celibacy, denial of the priesthood to women, birth control, abortion, homosexuality, masturbation, and other topics are perpetuated and defended by councils and papal decrees because it would be unthinkable to admit that the church has been wrong in the past. American priests are ordered to speak forcefully on these matters from the pulpit and to teach them vigorously to their congregations. This is a difficult thing to do for many priests. Therefore, they either ignore what the Pope says, or they soft-pedal what he commands. Wills paints the dilemma of the modern American priest when he says,

> The very fact that the intellectual level of the church has been raised makes it harder for a priest to swallow the scriptural fundamentalism reverted to by Rome when it claims that priests must be celibate or that women can-

not be priests. The cartoon version of natural law used to argue against contraception, or artificial insemination, or masturbation, would make a sophomore blush. The attempt to whitewash past attitudes toward Jews is so dishonest in its use of historical evidence that a man condemns himself in his own eyes if he tries to claim that he agrees with it.[5]

Pastors suffer from a fear of being honest with their ecclesiastical authorities and with their congregations and this presents a dilemma. Do Roman Catholic priests who love their congregations risk the wrath of Rome and removal from their parish by being honest, or do they pretend not to hear what the Pope demands? Do Protestant pastors hide their biblical knowledge in order not to disturb their congregations and risk being asked to leave, or do they find some kind of accommodation with the people they are called to lead?

It would only be fair to point out that pastors are not alone in confronting this problem of dishonesty. In talking with a high school teacher about this difficult situation, he reminded me that history teachers are faced with the same problem. The textbooks from which they are required to teach are deeply flawed and sometimes deceitful and yet to depart from the text is to court disfavor with the school administration. In his book *Lies My Teacher Told Me*, James W. Loewen

begins Chapter 11 with two quotes[6] referring to those
who write history texts:

> When you're publishing a book, if there's
> something that is controversial, it's better to
> leave it out.
> – Holt, Rhinehart and Winston representative

> There is no other country in the world where
> there is such a large gap between the sophisti-
> cated understanding of some professional histo-
> rians and the basic education given by teachers.
> – Marc Ferro

The problem of dishonesty is epidemic. Historians
lie, politicians lie, doctors lie, executives lie (as in the
case of the Firestone tires on Ford SUVs in 2000),
workers lie, parents lie to their children, children lie
to their parents – the list could go on and on. We live
in a world where truth is in short supply. Thus, it
would seem that pastors are simply doing what everyone else is doing and in a sense that is true. One
might argue that no one forces clergy to lie. They,
like history teachers and others who find it hard to
maintain their integrity on the job, could simply tell
the truth and suffer the consequences. Actually, some
would argue that abuse only occurs when a pastor is
harassed or punished for telling the truth. And there
is always the option of leaving the ministry and going

into some other profession – a choice which many pastors have taken.

So why am I suggesting that clergy are abused in a unique way by the pressure from higher ecclesiastical authorities and influential members of their congregations to mislead and withhold vital information from the people they serve? The answer lies once again in the ambivalent nature of religion. Along with the pressure to bend the truth comes the opportunity to help people discover the redemptive power of God's love. Along with the necessity to be less than honest comes the possibility of building ministries of service to the community and the world. Because the church is neither all good nor all bad, idealism must be abandoned for a more practical approach.

The trouble is that many pastors are idealists: they serve one who did not give in to the pressures which were placed upon him and who died for his honesty; they serve one who said, "You will know the truth and the truth will make you free" (John 8:32). Deep in their hearts they know that is true. They are a part of an institution which up until recently was looked to for moral leadership. When pastors are forced to lie or withhold the truth in order to keep ministering to people they love, they feel that they are not only betraying themselves, but also the one who called them, and the world to which they are ministering. Many clergy find that betrayal hard to live with, despite the fact that they believe the good they do out-weighs their lack of honesty.

If the church is to regain its moral leadership, it must relieve the burden of dishonesty from its pastors. This will take a threefold effort. Higher judicatories must be willing to stand up to those who hold the church captive to a long-outdated theology and understanding of scripture. Lay people must be trained in modern methods of biblical research, and they must be helped to see that the relationship with God they seek is not a matter of dogmas and doctrines, but rather a living relationship with a mystery that can never be contained in words. Finally, pastors must be willing to risk being honest with their congregations – they must risk speaking the truth in love. If that could happen, a great burden would be lifted from many pastors.

Abuse is present in every profession and to speak of abuse of clergy is not to imply that others do not also suffer. It is important, however, to remember that there are forms of abuse which we have explored in this chapter that are unique to clergy. It is also well to remember that clergy have more than an intellectual or monetary investment in their work. The faith of clergy is part and parcel of their work. When clergy are abused, they are being hurt by the people or institution to which they have devoted their lives and they often feel abandoned by God as well. When lay people are abused in their jobs, they can find solace and comfort in their religious community and in worship. Clergy do not always have spiritual havens to which they can retreat. Clergy who are abused have difficulty finding spiritual strength in the community of faith which they serve and many times they feel isolated and alone in their hour of distress. This is why it is imperative that pastors build support groups beyond their own congregations, groups that can minister to them if they find themselves in an abusive situation. It is also imperative that spouses of pastors develop friendships and spiritual soulmates to whom they can turn in times of trouble.

In the end, however, I am convinced that the abuse of clergy can be addressed best by lay people within each congregation who become aware of the problem and are willing to encourage pastors to share their deepest biblical insights, who honor the role of the prophet and are willing to defend the pastor's obligation to speak God's word of warning to the congregation, who take a close look at the pastor's compensation and challenge their fellow members to pay the pastor an adequate salary, who change their view of the pastor's spouse and expect no more of that person than they would of the spouse of a doctor or lawyer or any other professional person.

If I find any ray of hope about this subject, it comes in a portion of a commencement address delivered by Will Spong to the graduating class at the Episcopal Seminary of the Southwest in 1998. Will told how the Diocese of North Carolina in 1961, after much heated debate, finally voted to allow little black boys to attend the diocesan conference center. Soon after that decision, the rector of St. Peter's Church in North Carolina preached a sermon calculated to offset the "foolishness" of the action of the Diocesan Council and mollify influential members.

In his sermon, the rector called for gradualism and waiting and time. He exploited with fear and threats of miscegenation, mongrelization, and matters of that type. He talked about blue birds and red birds and trees as dwelling places of separation and division. It was a sermon that played to the sentiments of many Southerners of that time.

What intrigues me and gives me hope is what happened after that sermon. Will describes it this way:

> Five members of the vestry of that church asked to meet with Henry Egger, the rector. He looked forward to the meeting, expecting them to be proud of him since he had pleased them. It was a peculiar moment. They said: "Henry, we believe it is fair to say that all of us here are segregationists, we are afraid of integration, we have no experience in racial equality, we are terribly uncomfortable. We believe our way of life is the American way. But, Henry, even though we believe that and it accords with our thoughts, don't tell us that it is of God,

because we know better. It is a matter of shame for us and the Gospel, and we are convicted by that. But do not, Henry, do not tell us that our actions are in Christ Jesus because we know they are not. For your sake and for the sake of the Gospel, be a good priest, Henry, tell us about God. Do not sacrifice yourself to social convention and political expediency. God's love for his [*sic*] children surely helps us to know that."

In the final analysis, the abuse of clergy can best be addressed by dedicated, caring, biblically literate lay people in each parish who are willing to speak out, who are willing to challenge the preacher to be honest, to be a prophet. It can be best addressed by lay people who are willing to provide a livable wage for the pastor and his or her family; by people who are willing to refute those who spread idle, false, or malicious rumors; by people who are willing to take some of the burden off the pastor so that he or she can have time to teach and preach and care for those who are hurting within the congregation and the community. Clergy abuse can best be addressed by lay people who insist that the pastor be given time off to rest and reflect and grow as a person and a spiritual leader. Informed and compassionate lay people hold the key to combating clergy abuse and they must rise to the challenge.

8

THE THEOLOGICAL
ROOTS OF ABUSE

Abuse is not just the act of a few who are mentally deranged or monstrously evil. All of us are abusive to one degree or another, just as we are all more or less abused. When we look for the root cause of abuse, then, we are looking for something that is common to all of us.

James Poling suggests that power is the common factor which all human beings and institutions possess, and that the corruption or misunderstanding of that power is the major cause of abuse.

> *Power* is a complex term with personal, social, and religious connotations. At a personal level, all persons have some power by virtue of be-

ing alive, along with an inner drive to use this power to become all they can be. Some are denied the chance to exercise their power because of oppression. Others use their power for destructive ends. Society dictates how power is distributed. Institutions and ideologies determine who has privilege to be dominant and who must defer. Some persons are given great power to make choices for themselves and other people and are protected from the consequences of their choices. But many are denied the power to control even their own bodies and minds, and their choices are circumscribed by others. These inequities create the occasion for abusive behaviors and unjust power arrangements.[1]

We all possess power, but it is unevenly distributed and thus the stage is set for all kinds of abuse of individuals by other individuals and by institutions. In a perfect world, those with more power would share it with those who have less power and would protect the less powerful from those who would take advantage of them. However, in a very real and imperfect world, the powerful often use their power to gain even more control over the less powerful, taking away what little power they have.

The examples are obvious: relatively helpless and defenseless children are abused by more powerful parents; women are dominated, controlled, and abused by physically stronger males, aided and abetted by society's approval; minorities are abused by majorities; laity are abused by clergy and by institutional religion which claims the power of God to condemn those who disagree or who challenge a particular doctrine.

It is human nature, and the nature of institutions, to arrogate power to one's self, to gain control over other persons or groups. Abuse, then, will continue to increase until society protects the powerless, until someone, or some institution, leads us to a new understanding of power. Fortunately, society, through the legal system and the changing of public opinion, has taken some significant steps in the last decade to safeguard those who cannot defend themselves.

However, the most effective corrective to abuse will come from a change of heart. It will come as the Christian faith reassesses its understanding of power and teaches its adherents a radically new way of looking at this crucial concept. This reexamination would lead Christianity, I believe, to move from a concept of power that encourages and fosters abuse, to an understanding of power that encourages sharing and the empowerment of others.

To get to this new understanding of power will require a theological revolution, because our present concept of God and of salvation is based upon the idea that God uses divine power to dominate and control humankind rather than to empower us. I contend that this is not what the Bible ultimately teaches, but it is what institutional religion has led its followers to believe.

Look with me at some of the teachings of the church and you will see what I mean. In the Book of Genesis, we are told that God said, "Let us make humankind [often mistranslated "man"] in our image, according to our likeness; and let them have dominion over the fish of the sea, and over the birds of the air, and over the cattle, and over all the wild animals of the earth, and over every creeping thing that creeps upon the earth" (Genesis 1:26). Then the biblical commentator adds, "So God created humankind in God's image, in the image of God, God created them; male and female God created them" (Genesis 1:27 – my paraphrase based on the NRSV). The intention of God was that men and women should share equally in the task of being co-creators with God, and in the benevolent management of all the rest of the created order.

Christianity, however, has basically taught its adherents that God intended men to be superior to women and that nature and other creatures are to be dominated and controlled by *man* solely for the benefit of *mankind*. This teaching has made possible the rape of nature and of women by men whose power comes not only from their physical strength, but from ecclesiastical authority and from a society which has been controlled for centuries by men. In this misconception of biblical revelation, God has established a hierarchy with God at the top, followed by men, then women, then children, and, finally, the rest of creation. And despite passages which very clearly teach otherwise, the church has taught that those at the top of this chain of command have the right and obligation to force their will upon those who are beneath them, because they are inferior and must be dominated and controlled for their own good. Thus, the church through its theology has set the stage for an unquestioned power structure which leads to terrible and destructive forms of abuse.

Abuse is also encouraged by a theology that portrays a God of limitless and self-serving power: a God who wipes out all humankind and all the creatures of the earth except for one family and one pair of each kind of animal and bird because human beings didn't live up to divine expectations – a God who conspires with a chosen people to destroy cities and peoples in battle in order to further the divine agenda – a God whose anger consumes those who are not completely obedient and submissive – a God who must have a pound of flesh (even the flesh of God's own sinless son) in order to satisfy divine honor or justice. The picture of God put forth in the official teachings of the major denominations of the Christian faith depicts a God of absolute power and authority who is to be obeyed not out of love and gratitude, but in fear and trembling by all the rest of creation.

Abuse, then, is most likely to occur when you have a hierarchy of power established, maintained, and presided over by a divine monarch whose absolute dominion cannot be questioned. But there is one thing more to add which makes abuse inevitable – a theology which teaches that all human beings are depraved and sinful because of the act of an original couple who rebelled against divine authority. The doctrine of original sin and the atonement which it necessitated has done more to further abuse than any other doctrine, because it throws the whole concept of divine power into a negative mode. From that moment of disobedience at the very beginning of the human race, human beings, we are taught, fall under divine judgment and are powerless themselves to atone for their insult to God's honor. They must be rescued, then, by a perfect person who is willing to give his life to satisfy divine justice or honor. Because there is no perfect human being to serve as the ultimate scapegoat, God sends the God-Man to pay the penalty for human disobedience and to save all those who are willing to bow down and pay homage to him.

This doctrine of the atonement makes God sound gracious, but, in reality, it is based upon law, not grace. The official doctrine of the atonement which was first spun out by Anselm in the 11th century and only slightly modified by the various leaders of the Refor-

mation, and which is still found in the creedal statements of most churches, is the product of a legalistic
mindset which is based on power and control. It plants
firmly in our minds a picture of ourselves as worthless creatures, immobilized by sin, incapable of anything good, wholly dependent upon God for everything. It also pictures a wrathful God who must be
satisfied by a human sacrifice before being willing to
accept human beings into divine fellowship. Anselm's
doctrine of the atonement describes in frightening
terms the consequences which await those who fail
to submit to the conditions for that fellowship. It is
obsessed with sin, condemnation, and hell. The major function of the Christian faith becomes one of
helping believers avoid hell and divine wrath. If there
is any joy in the Christian message that is found in
hymns, liturgy, and sermons, the joy is in the fact that
God has deigned to save us, worthless creatures, from
the eternal punishment which we so grievously deserve.

In addition, this theory of the atonement gives
rise to great power for those who are the interpreters
of the faith and who claim, as God's representatives,
to have the final word as to what is acceptable to God
and what is not. If a particular branch of the faith can
convince its members that it knows what must be
done in order to be saved and that its path to salvation is the only way, that group will hold great power
over its followers. To have the keys to the kingdom of

God is to have awesome power, and the ability to control and abuse almost at will. The same could be said of any charismatic leader who claims the same kind of special revelation from God, or the unique ability to interpret scripture. That person, as has been demonstrated again and again, can demand unquestioning loyalty from his or her followers who feel that any kind of dissent will bring down divine wrath upon them. The threat of hell becomes a great club used to beat people into submission.

We should not be surprised, then, to find that those who want to control their followers and force uniformity of thought rely heavily upon authority and a power structure which allows them to control and dominate through fear and terror. The truth of the matter, as I have stated earlier, is that all religious groups use fear or manipulation to some extent. There is no such thing as a non-abusive religion, but there are faith communities that have become aware of the danger of their own abuse and that strive to minimize that abuse. The key to turning away from abuse, as much as possible, is found in a new understanding of power, both God's power and human power.

The power of God, as depicted in the long view of biblical history, is not the power to condemn and destroy. Instead, that power is demonstrated in the patient love of God which works with all of creation to bring forth the best that is possible in humanity and creation. It is the power of weakness, the power of long-suffering love and concern for all life on this planet and throughout the universe. God's power is a positive force that enables human beings to rise to their full potential. It is concerned not with punishment, but with rehabilitation and rebirth. God's power works its change in individuals and society not through fear, but through modeling what is possible, and then challenging us to aspire to be like that model. It teaches us not by demanding perfection or by negative criticism, but by positive reinforcement which praises our accomplishments and sets our sights on the next level of achievement, which becomes our goal. The greatest power is not the power to force one's will upon another, but the power to bring forth the best that is in another person – the power of love which enables us to trust God and ourselves and others once again.

Matthew Fox, a former Catholic priest, prolific writer, and director of the Institute in Culture and Creation Spirituality, points us in the direction of this new understanding of power in many of his books. Particularly in *Original Blessing* and *Creation Spirituality*, he challenges the ancient doctrine of original sin, with all of its negative baggage, and suggests that it must be replaced by a positive affirmation of the blessings of God, which begin at creation and are carried forth throughout all of life.

Fox reminds us that a religion based upon fear never leads to trust, which he correctly sees as the ultimate objective of faith. He argues passionately for the replacement of a religion of fear with a spirituality of trust. He writes:

> A devastating psychological corollary of the fall/redemption tradition is that religion with original sin as its starting point and religion built exclusively around sin and redemption does not teach trust...It teaches both consciously and unconsciously, verbally and non-verbally, *fear*. Fear of damnation; fear of nature – beginning with one's own; fear of others; fear of the cosmos. In fact, it teaches distrust beginning with distrusting of one's own existence, one's own originality, and one's own glorious entrance into this world of glory and of pain. Mahatma Gandhi understood the weakness in such a distrusting religious faith when he said, "What is gained through fear lasts only while the fear lasts." What if, however, religion was not meant to be built on psychologies of fear but on their opposite – on psychologies of trust and of ever-growing expansion of the human person?[2]

We need to recapture the joy of our faith in the affirmation that God loves us unconditionally, accepts us as we are, and enables us to become more fully the special and unique creatures which we were designed to be. We are not the totally depraved creatures that the theologian John Calvin pictured. We are wounded creatures, injured by the abuse of family and friends, and by circumstances. We are captives of attitudes and ideas that we have acquired in a variety of ways – attitudes that restrict our horizons and limit our ability to interact positively with others. We are people who have lost our ability to trust, who are fearful of letting others get too close to us because we have been betrayed too often by those most intimately connected to us. We are people who are filled with prejudice and insecurity who abuse and wound others because of fear or hatred. We are people who have not lived up to our potential. We are people who find it difficult to accept and love ourselves.

We are people in need of rescue and encouragement and empowerment. What we need, then, is not condemnation and threats of eternal punishment, but rather a constant and believable reaffirmation of our worth and value as unique beings made in the image of the Creator of the whole universe, beings capable of doing marvelous, creative, and wonderful things. The threat of hell, as an arbitrary place of punishment at the end of life, may temporarily deter some from doing destructive, evil things, but its effectiveness is solely based on fear and it rarely controls behavior or attitudes at the deepest level. On the other hand, to be rescued by a power greater than oneself from the reality of a very present hell of abuse or slavery, or from feelings of inferiority or worthlessness, or from any other captivity, can provide the motivation for a life lived in joyful and productive response to the source of that rescue.

Ultimately, we must ask whether God is jealous of divine power and position and is primarily interested in using that power to assure compliance to rules and regulations, or whether God is interested in using that power to help us develop our human capabilities to the fullest by removing the obstacles which prevent us from more nearly fulfilling our potential. In other words, is the biblical message *primarily* about maintaining God's honor and obeying God's rules, or is its *main theme* about God's great desire that God's creatures find fulfillment and joy and abundance of life, both now and throughout eternity?

I am firmly convinced that it is the latter rather than the former, and that when the Christian faith is presented in this light, it moves from abuse to blessing. Many passages of scripture point us in this direction. The most obvious is Jesus' statement concerning the purpose of his coming: "I came that they may have life, and have it abundantly" (John 10:10). When Jesus went back to his hometown and was asked to read scripture, he chose a passage from Isaiah which says,

> The Spirit of the Lord is upon me,
> because he has anointed me

> to bring good news to the poor.
> He has sent me to proclaim
>   release to the captives
> and recovery of sight to the blind,
> to let the oppressed go free,
> to proclaim the year of the
>   Lord's favor (Luke 4:18–19).

Then Jesus said to those assembled in the synagogue, "Today this scripture has been fulfilled in your hearing" (Luke 4:21).

When John the Baptist was imprisoned, he began to wonder whether Jesus was indeed the one sent from God to reveal the truth about God. So he sent his disciples to ask if Jesus was the one whom Israel had been looking for or should they expect someone else. Jesus replied, "Go and tell John what you hear and see: the blind receive their sight, the lame walk, the lepers are cleansed, the deaf hear, the dead are raised, the poor have good news brought to them" (Matthew 11:4–5).

The New Testament *does* contain harsh statements in which Jesus speaks of dire consequences for those who refuse to heed his message. But a majority of those warnings are directed at the religious leaders of his day who made a burden rather than a blessing out of religion. Jesus condemned the loveless, authoritarian approach to religion which characterized some of the Pharisees because he knew that it was negative rather than positive, abusive rather than healing. But remember that in the end, Jesus looked down even upon those who were so loveless, those religious leaders who had plotted his death and stirred up the crowds against him, and prayed, "Father, forgive them; for they do not know what they are doing" (Luke 23:34).

Jesus came to bring life abundant, not harsh condemnation, guilt, fear, and shame. His mission was to meet the physical, emotional, and spiritual needs of human beings, to be a champion of the poor and the powerless, to offer to all the limitless power of love. He accomplished that mission by taking the role of a servant, not a mighty king who could demand loyalty and obedience by might and position. Jesus died, not to satisfy the justice of God, but to demonstrate the length to which God would go to redeem the lives of those who were in bondage and fear. This way of salvation has always seemed strange and unbelievable to those whose only understanding of power is the ability to force one's will upon someone else. The apostle Paul caught the irony of it when he said that the power of God was found in weakness and in death and in love.

So we come back to that matter of power. If we continue to insist on a religion of power in the usual sense, we will continue to promote abuse of all kinds because we set up the structures in which abuse can flourish. We perpetuate that pyramid of unequal power in which those above can dominate and control those below. However, whenever we move away from that old concept of power and begin to look at how God has used divine power, especially as it is revealed in the life and teachings, ministry, death and resurrection of Jesus, we find a radically new kind of power – a power we can trust and believe in because we see that it is being used for our benefit rather than the interests of the one who wields it. When we put our trust in that kind of power, we obviously seek no advantage over those whose power is less than ours, for we have committed ourselves to one who came to serve others rather than lord it over them. We become fellow servants with the crucified, rather than officials in the palace of the king.

Because we are fearful that others will take advantage of us and dominate us, we resist the biblical vision of power. And to be sure, there *will be* occasions when others will use us for a time. But the old ways of power have not worked. They have perpetuated great abuse and death and suffering. Isn't it time, then, to give the biblical vision a chance, to re-examine the objective of our faith, and to move in a new direction? In a rediscovery of the biblical vision of power lies the greatest hope for a less abusive world – a world where concern for one another replaces dominance and control, and where suffering and pain are greatly diminished.

9

WHEN ABUSE
FORCES
YOU TO LEAVE

It is impossible to avoid being abused. We are abused by our parents, by our friends, by our spouses, by our children, by our associates, by the power structures of society, and by religion. Being aware of this potential for abuse is one of the best defenses against being injured too badly. When we recognize that good and bad are found in every relationship, we can choose to accept that which blesses and enhances our lives, and, to the extent possible, refuse to allow abuse its way. Therefore, we do not have to sever the relationship and we can work within an imperfect system.

However, all of us know that there are times when it is necessary to remove ourselves, either temporarily or permanently, from an abusive relationship. Sometimes children must be removed from abusive homes and placed with foster parents. Sometimes women must leave an abusive spouse, either temporarily until the spouse receives counseling, or permanently if the spouse refuses to change. Sometimes we have to leave an abusive situation in our work and seek employment elsewhere. And sometimes *we have to leave the church* for a while or forever, in order to find a new understanding of ourselves and our relationship to a power greater than ourselves.

I was talking just recently with a young woman who told me that she was raised as a Roman Catholic. She was no longer willing to live with the guilt which she felt her religion had placed upon her. She was also questioning many of the pronouncements of her church, especially those related to homosexuality and abortions. She had not been to Mass for some time. As we talked, however, it was evident that she still loved the church of her birth. She began to explore the possibility of talking with a friend of the family who is a bishop, about her frustrations with the church. I feel quite certain that if that bishop listens to her and hears her doubts and concerns with an open mind, she will eventually find her way back to the faith of her childhood. But she will return much wiser and more able to accept the good without being too badly hurt by the bad.

The young man I wrote about in the chapter on child abuse – the one who was abused so badly in a Baptist orphanage – left the church for several years.

The emotional scars and the anger he felt made him uncomfortable in church. He saw the church in a totally negative way. However, in 1991, he saw some ministers demonstrating against the military action in the Persian Gulf and he began to see the church in a new light. He had been active for some time in a local peace and justice coalition and he began to see that the church could work for good even as it sometimes harbored great evil. Eventually, he found his way back to a Methodist church where he worships regularly. He knows now that every religious community is filled with people who bless and who abuse, and he is wise enough to work for that which enhances while trying to change by the gentle persuasion of love that which destroys.

I am convinced that many of those who are estranged from their religious communities could find a new and more productive relationship if they were to speak honestly with their pastor about their concerns; if they were to explore other religious communities which are open to honest questions, which honor a diversity of experiences of the holy, which nurture rather than condemn, which do reality testing in their teaching and preaching. In most cases, if people are willing to take the time and energy to look for a religious community where nurture outweighs abuse, it can be found.

However, having said all of this, I must address those who have been wounded too badly to ever find a meaningful relationship to God within the institutional church. For some people, the time comes when they must leave the religious community in which they were raised, because the pain of staying is too great and stands in the way of a meaningful relationship with God. Let me tell you about three people who ultimately found it necessary to leave their faith family of origin.

James Newton Poling introduces us to Karen in his book *The Abuse of Power.* Karen was repeatedly molested by her father during her childhood. Later in life, she was raped by an acquaintance, a nationally recognized minister who was well-known and respected by the ecumenical church. Both her father and the minister who raped her obtained her silence through threats and intimidation. When she tried to confide in her pastor, he made sexual advances toward her himself and she withdrew more deeply into her state of denial. In order to cope with the trauma of incest, rape, and rebuff, she sought sanctuary in the busyness of a doctoral program. Her body, however, would not allow this escape forever and she fell desperately ill.

About this time, her new pastor preached a sermon on anger and she sensed that here was a person she could trust. She went to him for counseling and he referred her to a therapist. Over a period of several years, with the help of the therapist, individuals, and a support group, she made considerable progress. Because of the sensitivity of her pastor and a support group within the church, she began the healing process.

However, Karen ultimately made the decision to leave the church with her pastor's blessing. Why? Because it was evident to her pastor and to Karen that she could not feel comfortable and safe within a place that held so many terrible memories. When she went into a room where, many years ago, she had attended Sunday school as a four- or five-year-old, she remembered how she had been taught to honor her father and mother, to trust that her parents would always protect her from harm. As Karen got in touch with her feelings, she was able to identify the anger she felt toward the church which had taught that parents are always right and that the feelings and needs of children must always be subordinated. She began to see that the church's identification of parents with God, especially a male deity with a human father, was a contributing factor in the absolute dominance and control which parents exert over children, and which men exercise in relationships with women. That realization and anger marked the beginning of her departure from the church.

The final decision to leave was prompted by two incidents. One Sunday, during the worship service, she was horrified to discover that one of the persons who was serving Communion was the former pastor who had made sexual advances toward her when she came to him for counseling. She sought out a member of her support group after church and went to a quiet place where she sobbed and sobbed. Two weeks later, Karen was talking with a gentleman who mentioned the need to support a group of missionaries who were feeding the hungry in a Third World country. As he named the missionaries, Karen realized that one of them was the man who had raped her and demanded her silence.

After this second incident, Karen became aware that she must leave. She said, "The church was not a place for me. I could not feel safety or find peace in a place where the innocent cry inwardly with despair and the perpetrator is uplifted. I was convinced that I could never feel safe within the walls of this church. I appreciate my current past pastor, for he has been one of the gentle souls who has guided me in the past four years…He felt my pain and understood my need to leave."[1]

The church had both abused and blessed Karen. On the one hand, it had wrongly taught that parents are infallible and are always to be trusted as agents of a good God. It had perpetuated a patriarchal system in which male parents are not to be questioned and males in general are not called to account for the sexual abuse of women. On the other hand, a gentle and sensitive pastor had opened the door to healing through a sermon, patient listening to her story, and referral to a competent counselor. The church had also provided a select group of people who gave her unconditional love and support.

In the end, however, the trauma was too closely associated with the church for Karen to ever feel safe in its worship or fellowship. Therefore, she had to leave. Her pastor wisely and lovingly supported her need to go, without guilt or fear. That was the greatest gift he could offer and it is one which *we* must be willing to offer to those who have been so badly abused that they must seek other paths to God.

The wisdom of the pastor's gift is confirmed in Karen's present spiritual journey. While she was telling her story to a group of women, a member of the group said, "You seem to be a spiritual person. Who or what is your image for spiritual contact?" Karen was pleased that she was perceived as a spiritual person despite the fact that she was no longer active in the church. She shared with the questioner her most recent thinking on the matter of spirituality. She talked of a being who is neither male nor female, a being who is faceless, a being with spreading arms reaching out to her. She concluded, "I refer to it as the Great Healing Spirit. I like it. When I close my eyes in need to contact a spiritual being, this is what I image. It serves me well at this point."[2]

Karen had to leave the church because of sexual abuse which was too intimately connected with the religious community where she worshipped. Scott and Lydia Allen left the church because they felt deserted and abandoned by the religious community which had been a part of their lives since childhood. Their story was told poignantly by Jan Jarboe in *Texas Monthly* magazine.[3]

Scott Allen was the son of a prominent Baptist minister. He married Lydia, the daughter of his father's associate. After the wedding, they headed for Golden Gate Baptist Seminary in San Francisco. While there, Scott served as a pastor and Lydia worked as a psychiatric nurse. She also sang in the choir and taught Sunday school.

In 1982, they were living in Pacifica, California, where Scott was pastor of a small Baptist church and Lydia was pregnant with their first child. The night before the baby arrived, Lydia complained of stomach pains and Scott drove her to the hospital. There she received a blood transfusion and with it a death sentence for herself; the child, Matthew, who was born the next day; and another son, Bryan, born two years later. The blood Lydia received was contaminated by the AIDS virus, but this fact was not revealed to the Allens until three years after the transfusion.

When Lydia and her sons tested positive for AIDS, they finally had an explanation for the illnesses which had plagued all three of them. It was a devastating discovery that was made even worse by what was to come.

Scott was now serving as associate minister of the First Christian Church in Colorado Springs. When he told the senior pastor of the church about the awful tragedy which had befallen his wife and sons, the pastor offered his sympathy. Then, a few days later he asked for Scott's resignation. People in the church found out about the disease that was ravishing Lydia and the boys, but rather than offer care, concern, and practical help, no one even called to speak to the Allens in their great distress.

The Allens moved to Dallas where Scott went to work for the Christian Life Commission. Ironically, his job was to find churches where AIDS patients could find acceptance, but he couldn't find a religious community in his denomination where his own family could worship and study. Individual Christians *did* help in a variety of ways, but the institutional church would have no part of them. Scott's father, Jimmy Allen, lamented the church's failure when he said to Jan Jarboe, "The greatest blow was the failure of the churches to welcome Lydia, Bryan, and Matt." He continued, "I did not think the church as an institution would go so far as to deny the touch of Christ to innocent children."

Abandoned and wounded by the religious abuse they had suffered, Scott and Lydia battled to find meaning for their lives and a relationship with God beyond the religious community to which they had given so many years of service. Lydia found meaning for her remaining days as she worked with a psychologist in Dallas to form a support group for HIV women.

She died not having time to sort out what she believed about God and no longer able to worship in the church of her childhood. But she still clung to her belief that she would be reunited with her children after death. Scott left the Christian church to become an Eastern mystic.

It is sad when the church betrays the trust people place in it. When people hear weekly that God is love and that God loves unconditionally, they expect to *experience* that unconditional love in the fellowship of those who profess to be followers of Christ. The church can never fully live up to that expectation, just as parents are never fully able to love their children unconditionally. But in most instances, parental love and the love of the church family is there for us when we need it most – when illness strikes, when death comes, when we lose our job, when life tumbles in. However, there are times, as with the Allens, when fear or prejudice or a judgmental attitude cause the church family to draw back from people just at the moment when they need love and support the most. When that happens, the wounds of rejection cut so deep that return to the faith community is difficult, if not impossible.

What people need in these circumstances is the reassurance that the presence and comfort of God is not limited to the institutional church. God meets us wherever we are – in the privacy of our own hearts; in a therapy group; in the acceptance of a caring counselor; in another form of religion, perhaps one quite different from the faith community which has been familiar to us all our lives. God asks that we forgive those who have wounded us, but God does not ask that we return to the place of our abuse if we find that we can no longer respect our abusers. In that case, it is better to move on with God's blessing and to seek an awareness of God's presence and healing power in an entirely new setting.

There are times when people must leave the church in order to escape memories which get in the way of their communion with God. And there is yet another reason for leaving. Father Leo Booth claims that for some people religion has become a drug, and, as with all addiction, it may be necessary to remove oneself from the source of dependency. In his book *When God Becomes a Drug*, Father Booth describes his own addiction. Booth grew up in a dysfunctional family filled with quarrels and physical violence often centering around religious arguments between his mother, who was Anglican, and his father, who was Roman Catholic. At age 13, he fell under the influence of an Anglican priest whom he describes as controlling, authoritarian, arrogant, demanding, selfish, ignorant, and masochistic. Yet very, very funny. Booth writes, "Today, I am able to understand that the drama of church ritual – which, as a male, I was privileged to carry out – became my first drug of choice. It provided me a safe place where I could escape my dysfunctional home life. I was being molded for the priesthood. My self-esteem depended on my being part of an authentic remnant within the Church of England, solemnly observing the strict ceremonial of the Mass, attaining purity through sacramental confession, and not tainting myself by associating with Protestants, the non religious, or girlfriends."[4]

The seeds of Booth's addiction were sown. He became addicted to a God of ritual who controlled people through fear, guilt, and shame. He also became addicted to alcohol. It was, in fact, an alcohol-related auto accident which opened his eyes to both addictions. As a part of his treatment for alcoholism, he was encouraged to recognize his primary addiction. He describes his moment of truth: "My God and the trappings of my religiosity had become a disabling crutch. My sobriety would depend on my rejecting religiosity and becoming a spiritual person."[5] Booth remained a priest, but the focus of his ministry shifted to counseling with addicts of all kinds.

It is a tragedy when religious abuse is so severe that the abused finds it necessary for mental and spiritual health to leave the religious community, either temporarily or permanently. However, it is even worse when the church compounds that tragedy by telling the abused that there is no salvation beyond the religious community. It would be much more appropriate for the church to own up to its own sinfulness and to ask forgiveness from those whom it has wounded so grievously. When the church is willing to admit that it is capable of religious abuse, that it is not infallible, that it has on many occasions changed its mind and its understanding of God and what God desires for humankind; when it is willing to humbly confess its failures; when it does not claim to have sole possession of the keys to the kingdom; then, the door is open for dialogue with those whom it has abused and there is the possibility that they can return to the religious community from which they have been alienated.

10

MOVING
BEYOND DESPAIR

As I described the outline and contents of this book to a friend, she said to me, "Why do you have to be so negative?" I thought the answer to that question was quite obvious. Abuse *is* negative! It is destructive, hurtful, and even life threatening. The results of abuse are not pretty. They scar and quite often those scars remain for a lifetime. When the scars can be removed, it is only with great effort over a long period of time. I hope I have made that point as forcefully as possible because the time has come for some honest discussion and some radical changes within the religious community.

However, I know what my friend was really saying to me by her question. She was reminding me that it is very easy to get so caught up in the negative that one loses sight altogether of the positive. Her comment brought to mind the experience of Philip Hallie, who spent years reading and thinking about human cruelty. In his book *Lest Innocent Blood Be Shed,* Hallie tells how he lost the capacity to see the good while immersed in the evil he was studying. He writes:

> For years I had been studying cruelty, the slow crushing and grinding of a human being by other human beings. I had studied the tortures white men inflicted upon native Indians and then upon blacks in the Americas, and now I was reading mainly about the torture experiments the Nazis conducted upon the bodies of small children in those death camps.
>
> Across all these studies, the pattern of the strong crushing the weak kept repeating itself and repeating itself, so that when I was not bitterly angry, I was bored at the repetition of the patterns of persecution…My study of evil incarnate had become a prison whose bars were my bitterness toward the violent, and whole walls were my horrified indifference to slow murder…Reading about the damned I was damned myself, as damned as the murderers, and as damned as their victims. Somehow over the years I had dug my-

self into Hell, and I had forgotten redemption, had forgotten the possibility of escape.[1]

Hallie's escape from the hell of negativism came in
the form of a short article he found one day which
described the heroic and compassionate efforts of the
people of a small village in southern France who hid
Jews during the Nazi occupation. As he read how the
pastors and people of this village risked their own
safety and security, and how they shared their meager food and shelter to save the lives of thousands of
Jews, he rediscovered the human capacity for goodness and was liberated from the hell which he had
constructed for himself.

As we read and talk about religious abuse, as we
are forced to admit how widespread, multifaceted,
and pervasive it is, there is the ever present danger
that we will be sucked into the same black hole of
despair which almost robbed Hallie of his capacity to
see and rejoice in the good. To show only the negative, hurtful side of religion would be as abusive in
the end as the other forms of religious abuse which I
have tried to bring to consciousness.

So I must return to the thesis which I stated in
the first chapter; namely, *that religion is neither wholly
good nor wholly bad; when we think of it as being totally
healthy or completely sick, we are not dealing with reality.*
If we deny that religion can be sick at times, we expose ourselves to the possibility of abuse and we blind

ourselves to the reforms that are necessary to improve the health of religion. But it is equally true that if we fail to acknowledge the tremendous good that comes from religion, we cut ourselves off from the blessings that can flow from a healthy faith and are in danger of throwing the baby out with the bath water. It is imperative, then, that we remember that although religion can be abusive, *it can also be life affirming;* although it can wound, *it can also heal;* although it can be dictatorial, *it also liberates and frees us to explore and expand our horizons;* although it has been guilty at times of teaching prejudice and exclusivity, *it has also taught many to love and to serve and to include.*

I was reminded of this positive, healthy side of religion very vividly by two incidents which happened just recently. The first incident occurred when two women in their 30s spoke to a group of older people in the church I was serving as an interim associate pastor. They were asked to share with this group what it meant to them to grow up in this particular church. Both women were brought to church when they were very small children and they have been a part of this same church for over 30 years.

They each began by recalling how, as children, they had felt loved and valued by many of the members of that congregation. As one of the women put it, she felt comfortable – comfortable enough to fall asleep on the pew during a worship service. This congregation became for both women an extended family. In that family, they saw examples of God's love expressed in acts of caring and serving others.

As young people they found not rigidity and authoritarianism, but rather an invitation to explore and to question and to look at controversial subjects. As one of the women expressed it, they were *not* constantly being told, "No, don't do that. Don't think that way." Instead, they were encouraged to think and to investigate many ways of expressing the faith. When the pastor of the church died suddenly of a heart attack, they learned to deal with death and grief and the inevitable questions which follow the death of a young, vigorous, and beloved leader and friend. They experienced the church as a fun place to be, an exciting place to grow and develop and formulate a belief system which they could claim for their own. They found in the music of the church a vehicle which both inspired them and brought them to new heights in their relationship with God.

These two women admitted that they had used selective memory as they recounted their experience of growing up in this particular congregation. There were undoubtedly negative experiences which they could have shared, but it was evident that for them the good far outweighed the bad, and that their experience of religion had been and continues to be a very positive one.

Just a day after hearing these women speak, I had a conversation with another woman. This woman had gone through a divorce in her late 40s which had left her shattered, lonely, and despairing of the future. She left her friends and family and moved to Austin to take a job and to begin life anew. She had no friends or support system, but having been active in her church in her previous place of residence, she began looking for a church home where she could find the support that would see her through those dark days. And she was not disappointed. She found in the church a place of acceptance and healing, a place of warmth and friendship, a place which demanded little while she recuperated, but which offered a time of reflection and renewal.

The experiences of these women reminded me of my own experience with religion. After my mother's death, my father remarried and at age nine I returned home to live with my father and stepmother, after living with an aunt and uncle for three years. I was uneasy and somewhat frightened by the move. Fortunately, my stepmother accepted me graciously and lovingly, and the transition back home went well.

But my stepmother did more than welcome me into her home. She also brought me to a small Presbyterian church in our town. There I found an extended family which accepted me with warmth and care. I saw the Christian faith modeled in the lives of people who genuinely cared about me and about others. I had fun and I learned the stories of the faith. I celebrated the great festivals of the faith and felt included in the history of God's people throughout the ages. I found acceptance, self-worth, and a measure of security which I needed very much in those crucial days of my childhood and youth.

In the years which have followed, I have found in a Presbyterian college and seminary the freedom to question the faith I was first introduced to in that small church, the freedom to develop my own understanding of that faith without rejecting those who first handed it on to me. I have been blessed by serving churches which encouraged me to raise questions which enabled them to expand their own understanding of the faith. I have been blessed by being surrounded by people who lived out their faith by showing loving concern for others within the congregation, and for those in need within the community.

As I look back over the years, I can cite example after example of healthy religion being lived out in acts of service to those in need. Over 25 years ago, the church I served began a modest food pantry which supplied food to a few needy families each month. Over the years that food pantry has grown into three pantries which now supply food to several thousand families each year. Like many other churches, our church also began a childcare center for children of working parents, because we wanted to provide a place where children would receive loving care and feel secure while away from their parents. Another church addressed the problem of child care from a different angle. It saw the need for care of latchkey kids and it began a program called Extend-A-Care, which provided after-school care for elementary children, on or near the campus of the schools they attend. That concern which began in one small church has blossomed into a citywide program which now serves thousands of children on 20 school campuses every day. Still another church began a breakfast program for the homeless in our city. The idea for the breakfast program was born when a group of women in a Bible study became convinced that God was calling them to do something for the homeless. They began by taking doughnuts each morning to an area where the homeless gathered hoping to find work. After several months of this ministry, they decided that more was needed. So they organized transportation to take the homeless to the fellowship hall of their church where they could receive a more adequate meal and use the showers and lavatories in the church to clean up and make themselves more presentable for job opportunities. In less than four years, that program has spawned two other successful efforts to address the considerable problem of homelessness in our city.

When we look at the long history of Christianity, we find that the same religion which became mad with power and greed after it became the dominant power in the West began with such a great concern for widows and orphans and the powerless that Tertullian exclaimed, "See how these Christians love one another!" The same religion which has been used by some to justify child abuse has also been responsible for condemning child labor practices and for other crusades to better the condition of children. The same religion which has been used by the wealthy to maintain their domination of the poor has also been the catalyst for revolts against existing power structures resulting in beneficial social change. The church across the centuries has built hospitals, started schools, fed the hungry, clothed the naked, built homes for the homeless, set moral standards for decency and honesty, and crusaded for peace and justice.

I am very much aware of the blessings of religion; and I am very much aware of its abusive side. I have felt it necessary to call attention to that abuse because it is there and because we who are a part of the church must admit it. But perhaps the best way to eliminate the negative is not to dwell upon it, but to identify what is good and healthy so that we can strengthen that aspect of religion. So let's conclude by looking at four indicators of healthy religion.

Healthy religion is grace-filled rather than legalistic. Legalistic faith is built upon the need to fulfill certain requirements in order to make oneself acceptable in God's sight. A grace-filled religion begins with the conviction that we are *already loved* by the Creator of all things. In the assurance of that love, we find the power and motivation to become more nearly the persons we were created to be. Grace-filled religion shifts the emphasis from ourselves and what we can do to improve ourselves, to God and what *God* can do to enable us to fulfill our destiny. It does not remove responsibility from us, but it assures us that we are not alone in our struggle to be obedient to the divine vision for life that has been given to us.

Much abuse can be avoided when religion moves from legalism to grace. Therefore, we need to ask ourselves whether our religion teaches us to live by grace or by law. If we find ourselves or our religious community talking often about rules and seldom about the spirit which stands behind those laws, this should be a red flag warning us that we need to think once again about the grace of God which frees us from the tyranny of laws and which empowers us to let love and compassion be the guiding forces in all that we do.

Perhaps grace can best be understood through an incident which a friend described to me recently. My friend took her daughter to see *Snow White* while their family was living in El Paso, which is on the border of Texas and Mexico. Before they entered the movie, they made the necessary stop in the women's rest room. As they entered the rest room, my friend noticed a Mexican/American girl, who seemed to be no more than six or seven, standing in front of a mirror. She was dressed in tattered shirt and jeans, her hair was stringy and unkempt, her arms were pencil thin. Not knowing what caused her to utter the words, my friend turned to her daughter and said, "Look, honey, *there* is a real princess!" As the little girl standing before the mirror heard those words, my friend knew why they had been given to her by a power beyond herself. The waif standing before that mirror broke into a smile that spoke volumes about the self-esteem which had been awakened in her in a moment of grace. If that self-esteem and the grace which prompted it can be nurtured in the years to come, it could significantly change the course of her life. When we move from the realm of law to grace, we have laid the foundation for the second sign of healthy religion.

Healthy religion promotes forgiveness rather than guilt. We are all in need of redemption and forgiveness. The evidence of our destructive thoughts and behavior is all around us. We are a broken people living in a broken world. That is a fact beyond contradiction. The problem comes when we dwell upon our brokenness and our guilt and fail to accept the reality and finality of God's forgiveness. To feel perpetually guilty is to deny God's grace. We are *forgiven* sinners and we need a religion that reminds us of that fact again and again.

Healthy religion takes sin seriously, but it is careful to distinguish between our basic alienation from God, and the actions and thoughts which have been labeled as sin. In drawing a distinction between "sin" and "sins," healthy religion helps us get at the root of our problem and saves us from feeling perpetually guilty about everything we do that does not measure up to our understanding of what God wants us to do. Only God can overcome the alienation which exists between us and our Creator. God gives us the courage to return to God by overcoming our fear and suspicion, and by enabling us to trust that God is good and cares about our well-being. God comes to us in love and enables us to identify the source of our rebellion and alienation so that we can be reconciled and live more nearly the life God intended for us. The sin of mistrust is dealt with by God, not by rejection, but by an encounter with love which moves us slowly from mistrust to trust, from faithlessness to faith.

We can eliminate a lot of religious abuse if we keep clearly in mind the distinction between sin and sins, because once we have been firmly rooted and grounded in God's love, which overcomes our *sin*, we see our sins (the acting out of our mistrust) in a different light. Now guilt brings to mind not an external threat of rejection or punishment, but an insight which reminds us that what we are doing is hurting ourselves or others or the world which God created. Guilt becomes a positive force that enables us to change direction, to do something different, to cease doing something which is harmful.

And because we are securely anchored in God's love, we can question the moral teachings of the church without fear of God's rejection. We can question whether some of the things the church has declared are sins really *are* sins in God's sight. Is it sinful to play cards, to dance, to drink, to masturbate, to take birth control pills, to wear make-up, to be a practicing homosexual, to have sex before marriage, to get a divorce, to remarry after a divorce. We may conclude that any of these are sins, *but we do not have to automatically think of them as sinful simply because the church has often branded them as such*. We are freed from the fear of condemnation which religion has often used to enforce its understanding of God's will. At the same time, however, we are given the responsibility to search for God's direction for our lives as we explore the scriptures, as we look at the teachings of other religions, as we take seriously the insights of modern research and wisdom, as we pray for guidance, and as we discuss with other members of our faith community what God would have us do. We are freed from the tyranny of authoritarian religion which presumes to speak for God, telling us what is pleasing and displeasing to God. But that freedom carries a heavy price. It demands of us the willingness to search diligently, by ourselves and in the company of other seekers after God, for the path that God would have us follow toward health and wholeness for ourselves and for all other beings on this planet.

When we move from law to grace and from an obsession with guilt to the freedom to search for God's direction for ourselves, we can take the third step toward healthy religion.

Healthy religion allows us to move beyond religion and a particular belief system to a deep and transforming experience with God. This experience draws us back into our religious community with a whole new understanding of the values and limitations of that community.

A former Catholic priest who now serves as director of an ecumenical urban ministry once said to me, "I had to leave my religion in order to find my religion." What I believe he meant was that he had to get beyond or behind the teachings and the cultural trappings of his religion to find the essence or the core of his faith which was a relationship with the reality which we call God – a reality which defies definition or encapsulation in doctrine or dogma.

Marcus Borg, in his book *Meeting Jesus Again for the First Time*, speaks of the same experience in a different way. He writes:

Until my late thirties, I saw the Christian life as being primarily about *believing*…Now I no longer see the Christian life as primarily about believing. The experiences of my mid-thirties led me to realize that God is and that the central issue of the Christian life is not believing in God or believing in the Bible or believing in the Christian tradition. Rather, the Christian life is about entering into a relationship with that to which the Christian tradition points, which may be spoken of as God, the risen living Christ, or the Spirit. And a Christian is one who lives out his or her relationship with God within the framework of the Christian tradition.[2]

The Christian life is not about believing the right things. If it were, we would all be in great trouble trying to choose among the multitude of conflicting things different church groups have taught are essential for salvation. We would be in a constant state of anxiety worrying about whether we were believing exactly the right doctrines and avoiding false teachings. We would be putting our trust in a belief system rather than in the grace of a God who is beyond our ability to comprehend and who bids us to relax and to live joyfully in the assurance of God's love for the whole world.

When we can finally move beyond putting our trust in a particular belief system or creedal statement, we are freed to explore all the efforts of human beings to talk about God and God's activities in the world. We will find in them guidance and direction for our thinking about God, without falling into the trap of seeing them as completely accurate descriptions of God and God's will for us and for our world.

We can honor those who have struggled to under-stand who God is and what God is doing in our world and we can learn from them. We can use their in-sights to question our own understandings of God while recognizing that there is nothing infallible about either their understanding of God or ours. God is beyond the human ability to describe in words or belief systems. When we admit that, we are set free to learn from all who have gone before us and from our contemporaries without putting our ultimate trust in any system of belief.

When we move beyond belief to a relationship with God, we are freed to take the final step toward healthy religion.

Healthy religion allows us to move beyond exclusivity to see in other religions an effort to contact a reality and power which gives meaning to life, a reality which enables us to live more effectively with ourselves and others. Healthy religion recognizes that all religions have something important to teach us and that our own faith is strengthened when we look at how others have come to see the ultimate Reality of the universe. As we move from trust in a particular belief system to an open relationship with that ultimate reality we call God, we begin to see that this is the goal of many religions and of the great religious figures of the world.

For centuries, we in the West were not exposed to the insights of Eastern religions. We thought other religions were inferior to the Christian religion. In the last 50 years, however, we have had more contact with other religions. The more we come to know them and their adherents, the more we come to realize that they represent not something inferior but simply another path to that relationship with God which we all seek.

As we learn about other religions, we begin to see the vital role that religion, despite all its faults and failures, plays in addressing our deepest needs. Huston Smith, in his classic work *The World's Religions*, speaks to this point when he says, "authentic religion is the clearest opening through which the inexhaustible energies of the cosmos enter human life. What then can rival its power to inspire life's deepest creative centers? Moving outward from there through myth and rite, it provides the symbols that carry history forward…"[3] Smith reminds us of what Justice Holmes was fond of saying: that *religion, however small its successes, is at least at work on the things that matter most.*

That affirmation of Supreme Court Justice Oliver Wendell Holmes (1841-1935) provides a fitting conclusion for our discussion of religious abuse, because it reminds us that no matter how corrupted and abusive it may become, religion is not something we can discard without losing an indispensable communal source for understanding life and reality. Religion has to do with the things that matter most to each of us and to the world in which we live. Therefore, our task is to recognize and discourage religious abuse where it occurs while doing our best to foster and nurture those aspects of religion which are life-giving and life-sustaining. Religion is neither all bad nor all good and when we recognize that fact, we can get on with the task of working with God to make it as healthy as it can be.

POSTSCRIPT

When Martin Luther challenged the abuses of the church of his day, he nailed 95 theses to the Castle Church door in Wittenberg. He wanted to debate these abuses with the religious hierarchy. Unfortunately, his challenge was met with condemnation and, ultimately, with banishment from the Roman Catholic Church.

In a way, I wish that my challenge to the abuses of the church was as straightforward as Luther's. Today the church is splintered into hundreds of denominations. There is no central authority with which to lodge a complaint. Furthermore, there is much more local autonomy in each church.

However, that may be an advantage. Change rarely comes from those in positions of power. If the issue of religious abuse is going to be addressed, it will be because people like you are concerned enough to do something about it. If your heart has been touched and your concern raised by what you have read, I invite you to share this book with others. If you are a layperson, I invite you to give your pastor a copy and discuss it with him or her. If you are a pastor, I invite you to recommend this book to your lay folk and arrange to study it with them. Change will come only as consciousness is raised and as a significant number of people begin to work to make the church a less abusive, more healing and healthy place for all.

ENDNOTES

CHAPTER ONE

[1] Wayne E. Oates, *When Religion Gets Sick* (Philadelphia: The Westminster Press, 1970), p. 16.

[2] Ibid., pp. 17–18.

[3] Gregory Baum, *Religion and Alienation: A Theological Reading of Sociology* (New York: Paulist Press, 1975), p. 62.

[4] Ibid., pp. 62–63.

[5] Howard Clinebell, *Well Being* (San Francisco: HarperSanFrancisco, 1992), p. 25.

[6] Ibid., p. 24.

[7] Scott Peck, *The Road Less Traveled* (New York: Touchstone, Simon & Schuster, 1978), p. 206.

[8] David Johnson and Jeff VanVonderen, *The Subtle Power of Spiritual Abuse: Recognizing and Escaping Spiritual Manipulation and False Spiritual Authority within the Church* (Minneapolis: Bethany House Publishers, 1991), p. 20.

CHAPTER FOUR

[1] Richard R. Hammar, Steven W. Klipowicz, and James F. Coble, *Reducing the Risk of Child Sexual Abuse in Your Church* (copyright 1993 by Church & Tax Report)

[2] Jason Berry, *Lead Us Not into Temptation: Catholic Priests and the Sexual Abuse of Children* (New York: Doubleday, 1992), p. xx.

[3] Phil Quinn, *Spare the Rod: Breaking the Cycle of Child Abuse* (Nashville: Abingdon, 1990), pp. 156–157.

[4] Ibid., p. 157.

[5] Philip Greven, *Spare the Child: The Religious Roots of Punishment and the Psychological Impact of Physical Abuse* (New York: Vintage Books, 1992), pp. 39–40.

[6] Ibid., p. 49.

[7] Donald Capps, "Religion and Child Abuse: Perfect Together," *Journal for the Scientific Study of Religion* (March, 1992), p. 8.

[8] Quinn, *Spare the Rod*, pp. 163–164.

[9] Capps, "Religion and Child Abuse," p. 13.

CHAPTER FIVE

[1] Jenny Miller, *Church and Society* (September/October, 1991).

[2] Mary Daly, *Beyond God the Father: Toward a Philosophy of Women's Liberation* (Boston: Beacon Press, 1985), pp. 21–22.

[3] Ibid., pp. 33–34.

[4] Johanna W. H. van Wijk-Bos, *Reformed and Feminist* (Louisville: Westminster/John Knox Press, 1991), p. 66.

[5] Ibid.

6 Ibid., pp. 36–37.

7 Marcus J. Borg, *Meeting Jesus Again for the First Time: The Historical Jesus and the Heart of Contemporary Faith* (San Francisco: HarperSanFrancisco, 1994), p. 57.

CHAPTER SIX

1 Hans Küng, *Theology for the Third Millennium: An Ecumenical View* (New York: Doubleday, 1988), p. 227.

2 Ibid., p. 209.

3 *Insight: A Journal of the Faculty of Austin Seminary* (Fall 1991), p. 9.

4 John Hick, *God Has Many Names* (Philadelphia: The Westminster Press, 1980), pp. 17–18.

CHAPTER SEVEN

1 G. Lloyd Rediger, *Clergy Killers: Guidance for Pastors and Congregations Under Attack* (Louisville: Westminster/ John Knox Press, 1997), p. 8.

2 Marcia Clark Myers, *Presbyterian Outlook* (September 18, 2000).

3 Karen Armstrong, *Through the Narrow Gate: A Memoir of Spiritual Discovery* (New York: St. Martin's Press, 1981), pp. 154–155.

4 Borg, *Meeting Jesus*, p. 11.

5 Garry Wills, *Papal Sin: Structures of Deceit* (New York: Doubleday, 2000), p. 5.

6 James W. Loewen, *Lies My Teacher Told Me: Your American History Textbook Got Wrong* (New York: Touchstone, 1995), p. 271.

CHAPTER EIGHT

[1] James Newton Poling, *The Abuse of Power: A Theological Problem* (Nashville: Abingdon, 1991), p. 12.

[2] Matthew Fox, *Original Blessing: A Primer in Creation Spirituality* (Santa Fe: Bear and Company, 1983), p. 82.

CHAPTER NINE

[1] Poling, *Abuse of Power*, pp. 46–47.

[2] Ibid., pp. 47–48.

[3] Jan Jarboe, *Texas Monthly* (April 1993).

[4] Leo Booth, *When God Becomes a Drug: Breaking the Chains of Religious Addiction and Abuse* (New York: The Putnam Publishing Group, 1991), pp. 193–194.

[5] Ibid.

CHAPTER TEN

[1] Philip Hallie, *Lest Innocent Blood Be Shed: The Story of the Village of Le Chambon* (New York: Harper & Row, 1979), p. 2.

[2] Borg, *Meeting Jesus*, p. 17.

[3] Huston Smith, *The World's Religions* (San Francisco: HarperSanFrancisco, 1991), p. 9.

SUGGESTED
READING

I consciously chose not to write in depth about the subjects addressed in this book. My intent was to raise issues and areas of concern in the hope that you would be motivated to explore the subject more fully. To that end, I offer the following list of books, in addition to those quoted in the text, which expand and offer different perspectives on what I have said. I offer comments on some of the books where I believe they would be helpful.

CHAPTER ONE

Hall, Douglas John. *Christian Mission: The Stewardship of Life in the Kingdom of Death*. This title is out of print, but it's worth checking your library.

Wright, Lawrence. *Saints and Sinners: Walker Railey, Jimmy Swaggart, Madalyn Murray O'Hair, Anton LaVey, Will Campbell, Matthew Fox.* New York: Vintage Books, 1995. This is not a book about the church per se. It is a fascinating study of the strengths and weaknesses of six well-known religious leaders. As we look at these leaders, we can better understand the ambiguous nature of religion itself.

CHAPTER FOUR

Zarra, Ernest J. III. *It Should Never Happen Here: A Guide for Minimizing the Risk of Child Abuse in Ministry.* Grand Rapids, MI: Baker Books, 1997. This book can be used in alerting pastors and lay people to the dangers of child abuse in the local church. It is a good reference for committees working on child abuse policies for their church.

Capps, Donald. *The Child's Song: The Religious Abuse of Children.* Louisville: Westminster John Knox Press, 1995. As a follow-up to his article on religion's responsibility for child abuse, which I quoted in this chapter, Capps has written this book which treats the subject more thoroughly.

CHAPTER FIVE

Fortune, Marie M. *Is Nothing Sacred? The Story of a Pastor, the Women He Sexually Abused, and the Congregation He Nearly Destroyed.* Cleveland: The Pilgrim Press, 1999.

Ranke-Heinemann, Uta. *Eunuchs for the Kingdom of Heaven: Women, Sexuality, and the Catholic Church.* New York: Doubleday, 1990. Ranke-Heinemann is a German Catholic theologian who points out the abusive nature of the Roman Catholic Church's teachings on women and human sexuality.

McFague, Sallie. *Metaphorical Theology: Models of God.* Philadelphia: Fortress Press, 1987.

CHAPTER SIX

Cox, Harvey. *Many Mansions: A Christian's Encounter with Other Faiths.* Boston: Beacon Press, 1988.

Anderson, Gerald H., and Thomas F. Stransky, eds. *Christ's Lordship & Religious Pluralism.* New York: Orbis Books, 1983.

Hick, John, and Brian Hebblethwaite, eds. *Christianity and Other Religions.* Philadelphia: Fortress Press, 1980.

Smith, Huston. *The World's Religions.* (San Francisco: HarperSanFrancisco, 1991), p. 9. Huston Smith's book, *The World's Religions,* is cited in the endnotes for Chapter Ten but I want to remind the reader that this is the classic text for anyone who seeks to know more about the other religions of the world.

CHAPTER SEVEN

Haugk, Kenneth C. *Antagonists in the Church: How to Identify and Deal with Destructive Conflict.* Minneapolis: Augsburg Fortress Publishers, 1988.

Shelley, Marshall. *Well-Intentioned Dragons: Ministering to Problem People in the Church.* Minneapolis: Bethany House, 1994.

CHAPTER EIGHT

Fiddes, Paul S. *Past Event and Present Salvation: The Christian Idea of Atonement.* Louisville: Westminster/John Knox Press, 1989. This book is written for lay people as well as theological students. It is excellent for those who want to explore, in depth, the many ways in which the purpose of Christ's death has been understood across the centuries.

Kushner, Harold S. *How Good Do We Have to Be? A New Understanding of Guilt and Forgiveness.* Boston: Little, Brown and Company, 1996.

CHAPTER NINE

Enroth, Ronald M. *Recovering from Churches That Abuse.* Grand Rapids: Zondervan Publishing House, 1994.

CHAPTER TEN

Clinebell, Howard John. *Anchoring Your Well-Being: Christian Wholeness in a Fractured World.* Nashville: Upper Room Books, 1997.

Spong, John Shelby. *Why Christianity Must Change or Die: A Bishop Speaks to Believers in Exile.* San Francisco: HarperSanFrancisco, 1998. Bishop Spong calls for a new reformation that will move the church away from much of its abuse and toward a healthier understanding of God, away from morality that is outdated and unscriptural to a morality that is more humane and compassionate.

Other titles by Northstone Publishing and Wood Lake Books that stimulate conversation

JACOB'S BLESSING
Dreams, Hopes and Visions for the Church
DONNA SINCLAIR & CHRISTOPHER WHITE
A hopeful and inspirational vision of the future of the church. Video and study guide also available.
ISBN 1-55145-381-9

DYING CHURCH / LIVING GOD
A Call to Begin Again
CHUCK MEYER
Challenges those in the pews and outside the tent to renew the church.
ISBN 1-896836-39-9

RIDING THE ROLLER COASTER
Living with Mood Disorders
MARYA BERGEN
Practical tips that make it possible to live a full and productive life despite coping with a mood disorder.
ISBN 1-896836-31-3

LANGUAGE OF THE HEART
Rituals, Stories, and Information about Death
CAROLYN POGUE
Meaningful, healing ceremonies from those who have dealt creatively with death.
ISBN 1-896836-17-8

PART-TIME PARENT
Learning to Live without Full-Time Custody
CAROLYN POGUE
A one-of-a kind book that shares real stories of non-custodial parents. Useful for counselors and clergy.
ISBN 1-896836-23-2

PRECIOUS DAYS AND PRACTICAL LOVE
Caring for Your Aging Parent
JAMES TAYLOR
Practical advice on the changing relationship
with aging parents.
ISBN 1-896836-34-8

TWELVE SMOOTH STONES
A Father Writes to His Daughter about Money, Sex, Spirituality and Other Things that Really Matter
CHUCK MEYER
Real issues that adolescents face in user-friendly language. Gets the conversation started.
ISBN 1-896836-27-5

SECRET AFFAIRS OF THE SOUL
Ordinary People's Extraordinary Experiences of the Sacred
PAUL HAWKER
Firsthand accounts of life-changing spiritual experiences from a broad range of individuals.
ISBN 1-896836-42-9

SPIRITSCAPES

Mapping the Spiritual and Scientific Terrain
at the Dawn of the New Millennium

MARK PARENT

An overview and analysis of nine of the most significant
spiritual and scientific movements of our time.
ISBN 1-896836-11-9

PRAYER: The Hidden Fire

TOM HARPUR

Brings the broad theological perspective of prayer to the
personal level.
ISBN 1-896836-40-2

SIN: A NEW UNDERSTANDING OF VIRTUE & VICE

JAMES TAYLOR

Examines the fascinating origins and evolution
of all seven deadly sins.
ISBN 1-896836-00-3

WOOD LAKE
BOOKS
NORTHSTONE

Find these titles at any fine bookstore, or
call 1.800.663.2775 for more information.

Check our website www.joinhands.com

KEITH WRIGHT served as pastor for forty years in the Presbyterian Church USA. He received his Doctor of Ministry degree and the Distinguished Alumni Award (1992) from Austin Presbyterian Theological Seminary.

Since his retirement in 1993, Dr. Wright has served as an interim associate pastor at Westminster Presbyterian Church, Covenant Presbyterian Church, and University Presbyterian Church in Austin, Texas. When he is not busy with church activities, Dr. Wright enjoys photography, woodworking and working in his greenhouse.

DATE DUE
